arrive on *wave*

Collected Poems
Gil Ott

edited by Trace Peterson
Gregory Laynor
& Eli Goldblatt

chax
2016

ISBN 978 0 925904 91 1

chax press
po box 162
victoria, tx 77902-0162

Acknowledgement to Julia Blumenreich for her careful consideration of all aspects of the book, to Wendy Osterweil for her comments leading to decisions about art on the cover of the book, to Cynthia Miller for her consultation on the book, and to Benton Leitner for his careful proofreading.

Chax Press is supported in part by the School of Arts & Sciences at the University of Houston-Victoria. We are located in the UHV Center for the Arts in downtown Victoria, Texas.

Chax acknowledges the support of graduate and undergraduate student interns and assistants who contribute to the books we publish. In Fall 2016 our interns are Julieta Woleslagle, Sophia Kameitjo, Errin Maye, and Gabrielle Delao.

This book is also supported by private donors. We are thankful to all of our contributors and members. Please see http://chax.org for more information.

dedicated to the memory of

Gil Ott

Foreword

by Eli Goldblatt

It feels wrong to speak about Gil Ott's life in relation to his writing, but I'm going to do it anyway. He didn't talk much about personal issues for most of the first twenty years I knew him, and in his writing he avoided language that might encapsulate and contain ideas or people, including himself. Indeed, I couldn't encapsulate Gil in a story or a phrase if I wanted to. I think, however, a few thoughts about his life may help new reader to enter Gil's work, and I can't help but notice certain threads and trajectories in this volume. He was a poet, a political thinker in the arts, a conscious member of the disability community, and a sustained and sustaining presence in the lives of those who loved him. You could not predict the texture of his writing from any of these particulars, and his language does not settle into easy patterns no matter which of his books you encounter. Still, context may help some readers, and one goal of this collection is to gain a new audience for work that I regard as among the best of our generation.

He was a poet who lived out the rhythms and possibilities of language as tenaciously as anyone I know. He said in *Public Domain*: "The poem is public event, host to a multitude of private entries, a defined anarchy." He used the poem as the focal point for entering fully into a present neither oppressed by the past nor dominated by the future. This is the motive for the swift changes in mid-line and mid-stanza that align him with language poetry, though he never considered himself part of that group despite the many poets of the tendency he published. I think Gil's focus on presentness traces to a Buddhist poetics that he encountered with Steve ("Kush") Kushner in San Francisco in the early 70's. He later renewed his interest in Zen through conversations with Zoketsu Norman Fischer in the 90's while Gil was on fellowship at the Headlands Center for the Arts in California. Gil was always aware of the way language builds worlds around us, and he looked for holes and gaps by which we could escape conventional wisdom to create a larger, more compassionate music. Through both his journal *Paper Air* and Singing Horse Press, he developed a following that comes only to the best small press ventures, and yet what authors most got from publishing with Gil was not notoriety but the challenge he set us: to push the boundaries of what could be imagined in words.

Nearly in equal measure, Gil was a political thinker. Not that he cared much for party affiliations or spin control. But he thought about what made a block of people into a functioning community, what made a gang of do-gooders into a movement, what made a knot of poets into a real poetic force. He was particularly thoughtful about bridging a great gap in US culture: the connection between the arts and social justice. During his years with the Painted Bride Art Center, the non-profit organization where he worked for seventeen years, he founded programs to work through drama and poetry with homeless people, prisoners, school children, as well as anyone else who chose the arts as their means for questioning the taken-for-granted order of things. In one instance, he brought a playwright into a neighborhood where there had just been a murder of a kid from one ethnic group by kids from another group. The play that emerged from the months of development brought enemies together and forced people outside and in to confront the conflicts and contradictions of urban life. Gil knew that art does not belong on the top shelf, a fine scotch nobody is allowed to drink.

Gil told me near the end of his life that it was extremely difficult, once he began working for the disability support center called Liberty Resources, to accept himself as a member of the disability community. He empathized and worked for other people's freedoms, but at first he just couldn't see himself as disabled. I doubt any one moment changed that for him, but I know editing the collection *No Restraints: An Anthology of Disability Culture in Philadelphia* (New City P, 2002) pushed him in that direction. He recognized in that project that he had a significant "alignment" with people in wheel chairs, people who had been hospitalized for mental illness, people whose language seems garbled to others who think themselves more normal. In the introduction to *No Restraints* he said a community built on such identification could truly be called a "movement" because once "they have declared their alignment, their members must continue to move, that is to demonstrate and re-demonstrate" for equality and justice. He recognized that his nearly thirty-year struggle with the complications of kidney disease had been a formative element in his life and not a sign of personal weakness.

Gil lived in that hurt body and danced damn well inside it, creating beauty from his location. I think his own experience with illness helped make him so fiercely compassionate, so incapable of condescension toward anyone. You can see traces of a concern for the body in lines and utterances throughout the work. He's seldom explicit, but movement and physicality are choreographed elements that enter the poems: invitations to walk or dance or sing, notations of damage such as burns or twists or exposure. Early on, in "the children," we read:

> Call it the heat,
> our presence in disease
> and in beatitude
>
> that draws you toward the angel of perfection

In *The Amputated Toe*, he is nearly coy at first about the appendage that appears in the third section with the remark "You've been waiting for the toe to show up." Although beyond the title, he doesn't directly name his identification, I can't help but see that last book as his wicked little nod to membership in a culture he worked so hard to promote as development director at Liberty Resources Center for Independent Living.

Gil was here for those he loved intimately. Our most personal conversations occurred after we both became fathers. I cannot imagine a stronger, more sustaining love than that he held for his daughter Willa. They made art, told wild stories, and invented songs together. With Julia he had a marriage of profound companionship, respect, and caring, the sort of mutual relationship that friends take joy to witness. Julia and Willa were the best things that ever happened to Gil, and he sure knew it. But Gilbert Ott could also be cantankerous, irascible, and downright curmudgeonly. Like the time somebody at a party suggested Julia move their little dog Tucker so that he wouldn't get stepped on, and Gil growled, "Yeah, put him in the freezer." He walked Tucker many cold nights, but he wasn't going to give anybody the satisfaction of knowing that he **liked** living with all those animals Julia & Willa brought home.

I read *Public Domain* as a book that, among other functions, is processing the emotional closeness with Julia that he had never experienced with anyone else, testing the flex and failure of language in intimate as well as public quarters. *Traffic*, in my mind his most enduring book, tracks physical and emotional beings as they impinge and trail off the oscilloscope of a highly tuned psyche. Pact, one of the most expansive little books I know— resonant with Kafka's short stories or Lydia Davis's work today—strikes me as representative of his greater emotional openness to others at the end of his life. Increasingly he allowed the playful and humorous side of his personality to manifest in his verse as it did among family and friends. Witness, for example, that great comic scene in *The Amputated Toe* where the stage is swept clean except for a stick figure woman with a head of curls sitting before a pupa/toe the size of a football "flexing blindly on a platter." If you don't let yourself laugh at moments in this book, you miss a significant aspect of Gil's worldview.

I don't know if any of this will help new or old readers explore *A Defined Anarchy*. Many people who knew Gil as a friend in the neighborhood or at work have told me they find his poems difficult to read. Poets with a reading knowledge of the tradition from Stein to Bernstein more easily find pleasure and instruction from the disjunctions and leaps in his verse and prose. I hope more people make the effort to enter here because Gil would certainly insist you don't need a degree to read his work. I see a richly varied terrain in the poems and fiction collected here. One can experience the gentle daring of "the children"—where the first collection of criticism on his work took its title *the form/of our uncertainty*—or the tough eroticism and restless narrative voicings in *Public Domain*. I particularly prize the *I Ching* quality of *Traffic*—momentary perception in dialogue with a flat but compassionate spiritual commentary. When I read *Pact* again, I'm amazed at his ability to spark story and character from the barest sentences. The surrealist setting for poetic drama in *The Amputated Toe* (not to mention the ersatz German you can almost understand) remind me that the San Francisco street poet in Gil always intended his art to make things happen in this steep and disjointed world. He's an uncompromising investigator never satisfied with a definite plot line or a burnished phrase. Once you recognize Gil will simply not answer present quandaries with a "regimentation of meaning," you can settle back and enjoy his refreshing and mobile awareness on every page.

On Gaps, Embodied Activism, and Swerving Away from Statement: An Editorial Introduction

by Trace Peterson

I have never met Gil Ott. So what am I doing editing this book? Well for one thing, he is one of my favorite poets. His work is so moving and powerful—its odd, wayward beauty continually unfolds new meanings and surprises the more time I spend reading it over the years. I have participated in the editing of this collected poems, along with my co-editors Gregory Laynor and Eli Goldblatt, because I want everyone to read Ott's work and I think it is tremendously important. For another thing, Gil Ott is part of my poetic context. I have heard so many stories about him from poets who I consider friends and colleagues—Charles Alexander, CA Conrad, Norman Fischer, Ron Silliman, Bob Perelman—that I can see how he was the glue that held together and made vibrant a certain kind of poetic community in Philly from the 80s through the mid 2000s while maintaining a kind of maverick position in relation to available options. He did it all—poet, publisher, editor, curator of readings, and host—which is exactly how we all should be pitching in and contributing to a larger community as literary activists. This jack-of-all-trades poetic activist role that Gil Ott took up is one which I empathize with and value highly, having taken it up myself for various reasons during the past decade. I admire how Gil Ott was so personally invested and so powerfully independent. It boggles the mind trying to imagine the kind of commitment it must have taken for him to curate poetry readings that made a difference in his community, while publishing some of the most important books of his moment via Singing Horse Press, while published some of the most influential poems and poetics essays of his moment in his magazine *Paper Air* (Charles Bernstein's "Artifice of Absorption" comes to mind as a key example), while managing to focus on his own poetry and produce the magnificent body of work and the poetic vision that we see collected in this volume.

What do I love about Gil Ott's work? Let me try to count the ways. One of the most noticeable effects effects of his language is an intentionally disrupted, disarrayed quality. Achieved through play with syntax and sentence structure, and often resulting in a half-swallowed syntax like what is left over when parts of a text are erased in between the joints, this kind of gorgeous illegibility can be absorbing and hypnotic. It continually invites the reader in and then rebuffs them. The energy and emotion of the poems are not achieved through some kind of lyrical flights of the egotistical sublime—rather, they occur through the deliberate derangement of what seems to be everyday, casual talk that has somehow been split open and made glorious. The poems are supposedly accessible, engaging, and often charming, but it would be a challenge for anyone to do a simple precis of what just happened. Following one of his early self-imposed rules, "no statement," one can see how there is an ongoing sense of "seeking to unveil and build down"—of immersion in what is about to be said, which then continually swerves away from a message just slightly enough that the functional aspects of communication momentarily crumble and are continually partially reconstructed.

The author's body and its relationship to the shards of voice we can hear in the poems are important parts of the process throughout. As someone who became ill with severe kidney disease in the mid-70s before he even wrote his first book of poems, Ott is an author whose writing is complicated by the body, foregrounding the complexity of its furtively embodied elements, straining against the kinds of restrictions on that body that a lot of able-bodied writers and readers don't have. As a consequence, the figure of the writer limiting what is seen or how it is seen continually seems to complicate what is happening. One thing that Ott's poetry demonstrates is that no matter how abstract or seemingly improvisatory one's language becomes, it is still nearly impossible to keep the author's life, body, and political concerns out of the poem. These things persist because of how the body of language and one's experience of the body are intimately connected. So one of the rules may be "no statement," but part of the beauty of this work is how life—and the work as a form of life—are also so powerfully and undeniably present.

A key location where these two elements meet—the disrupted or disarrayed quality in Ott's writing and the way his bodily experiences persist and can't entirely be kept out—is in his use of gaps and how that use develops over the course of his oeuvre. Beginning in the early poems such as "Trio of the Approaching Life" in the late 70s, the author plays with multiple columns of text, a perspective which seems to understand the center of the poem as a kind of gap or hinge. Something evocative happens to reading and thinking across this gap horizontally. In a June 1981 letter to Eli Goldblatt, Ott refers to one of these early poems as a "2-voicer." So part of what he had in mind seems to be a movement toward opening up the voice of the poem from a single speaker to something more dialogic. By the time Ott reaches 1985, the first volume of *Traffic* (books 1 & 2) finds him shifting this horizontal gap to a vertical one—which also becomes a kind of call-and-response gap between poetry and prose. The "Traffic" poems constitute an important discovery for the poet and one of his most interesting accomplishments. The two modes, poetry and prose, run both chronologically forward, like a text and the commentary on that text, but they are also somehow able to be side by side, or parallel in their purposely inarticulate articulations.

I was in a NY hotel room discussing poetry publishing matters with Charles Alexander on the afternoon when he got the phone call that Gil Ott had died. I saw how much Ott's life and work had affected Charles and what a huge loss this was for him. I am very honored to have been included in working on this project with Gregory Laynor and Eli. I also understand that there are certain things I cannot presume in this situation. The title of this volume, for example, was selected by Julia Blumenreich and Eli after some debate. Among the other titles we had considered were "a defined anarchy" and "architect of the gap," but Eli and Charles and Julia assure me that "arrive on wave" is the best name for this book, and I take their word for it.

The organization of arrive on wave took a lot of time and attention to detail. Gathering all of Ott's poetry in one place turned out to be a larger task than any of us had anticipated. In addition to the noteworthy books like *Public Domain*, *Traffic*, *The Yellow Floor*, *Pact*, and *The Amputated Toe*, we found chapbooks from over the years (some of which had been self-published), and entire issues of journals dedicated to Ott's work, and we also found quite a few unpublished poems. We agreed at the beginning that it would make the most sense to arrange everything chronologically so that both readers already familiar with Ott and new to his work could see how changes and discoveries occurred in a timeline. Greg and I began by retyping all the books out into a larger document, but in the process of doing that realized that there were a lot of duplicate poems across different books and chapbooks. Ott sometimes republished certain poems in different books, trying to find the right context for them, especially in the early books when his style was the most restless and going through the most development. In some cases the same poem would appear in three different volumes, and I felt that kind of repetition would be distracting and get in the way of reading the collected. So in most cases, what we did is to include poems the first time they appear, in the first volume they appear, and delete the duplicates that appear in later books. This illuminates the timeline leading up to The Yellow Floor, because now we can see in what order some of those poems first happened that were later gathered in *The Yellow Floor*.

However, we made two exceptions to this "first appearance best appearance" rule for duplicate poems: Traffic and For The Salamander. Arguably Ott's most important sequence, or at least the one where he grew the most through the process of writing it, the Traffic poems originally spanned several different books, including Traffic (Books 1 & 2) from 1985 and Within Range from 1986, the former self-published by Singing Horse Press and the latter published by Burning Deck. Since all three books of the entire Traffic sequence had been already collected in one volume by Chax Press in 2001 in a version supervised by Ott himself, we opted to publish the whole final sequence together. The following list is the original timeline of all of Ott's books and chapbooks in chronological order:

Light Series (1978)
Maize (1979)
Trio of the Approaching Life (1980)
The Children (1981)
Poems from *Origin* 20 (July 1982) [overlaps with *For The Salamander* and *The Yellow Floor*]
Ladder from *Loot* 3:2, a supplement to *Spectacular Diseases Magazine* (July 1983)
Traffic (Books 1 & 2) (1985) [overlaps with 2001 complete edition of *Traffic*]
For the Salamander (1985) [overlaps with Origin poems]
Within Range (1986) [overlaps with 2001 complete edition of *Traffic*]
The Yellow Floor: Poems 1978-1983 (1987) [overlaps with *Origin* and *For The Salamander*]
Public Domain (1989)
Wheel (1992)
The Whole Note (1997)
Traffic (2001)
The Form of Our Uncertainty (2001)
Pact (2002)
The Amputated Toe (2006)

The volumes we removed because of repetition were *Traffic (Books 1 & 2)* and *Within Range*. There was also some overlap between the poems in *Origin* and various other books. In the instance of an overlap between *For the Salamander* and *Origin*, we opted to delete the earlier versions that had appeared in *Origin* because Ott had added additional material in the final version of *For The Salamander* which makes that chapbook feel like more of a piece, more like a self-contained serial poem in itself. Where overlap occurred between *The Yellow Floor* and *Origin*, we removed poems from *The Yellow Floor*, including "Symbiosis," which also appeared in both *Ladder* and *The Yellow Floor*, and the poem titled "The Yellow Floor" itself. Although Douglas Messerli's publication of *The Yellow Floor* via Sun & Moon Press was an important event, the book is like a mid-career selected poems that gathered some things but left out some earlier work, so I felt it would be arbitrary for us to maintain that collection in its entirety.

Our hope is that *arrive on wave* will help the people who loved Gil Ott and were influenced by him to remember him as the prolific, independent poet he was, and at the same time we hope this book will reach new readers who are just learning about Ott's work for the first time. At the end of his chapbook "Fugue," Ott included a section titled "About the Author":

> Wasn't that a tidy ending? Now you can go back to your business. What is your business, anyway? I'm very interested in you. Let me get closer to you so you can speak directly into my good ear. Does this bother you? Am I giving off an unpleasant odor? I've tried everything to get rid of it. Lotions, soaps, baths, powders. Do you have any suggestions? If you say it, I'll do it. I'm very fond of you, you know.

The playfulness is this section might look like your standard death-of-the-author argument at first glance, but I think it means something more from the perspective of literary community. Book publishing and design is often called an "invisible art" in the self-effacing sense that the labor one does is always in the service of the text at hand. Literary journal publishing, organizing readings, community activism—these too are "invisible arts." One does not undertake these activities because one wants to be "the star"—rather, the public role of poetry and community activism is something of a different nature enitrely. For this poet who was continually so modest and dignified about not claiming credit for the immense labor he did on behalf of poetry, our hope is that this book will give his brilliance as a writer a well-deserved spotlight—that it will result in a process whereby both readers who knew him and are just meeting him for the first time can all finally have a chance to wrestle with the multivalent affects and furtively embodied meaning of his words, allowing us, in a new way, to "get by the neck and think it."

Contents

Light Series

Self-published

1978

ROY G. BIV

we've seen
and so contained
sight.

but whose choice
deems this noon-flower red?
heat, great and overpowering,
threatens and so is bound:
red, yellow, green.

we are smaller. Stop
and take in the sun's full power
surrounds you. See
the brilliant tiger's jaws
to suddenly
too near.
whose fear?

PRISM

men and men
and on and on the fringe
dance without movement

so angled
is fans is to edge's
multiple flame.

from
light from light
the rings proceed
whose seat is
everywhere in

in from all points powerful.
break open the fruit and
see.

see needles
blades and the way
etch retina

so eyes slice
bring it in in
bits, figure
and ground.

now gather that
chrome that blanks
the upper choirs,
or beads
sharp star
revealing worlds,

not many but
lights one mind.

P RMIS E

punched, so
rain slants against humor

nights twitch at
grows winter winter
shunts them under
alien soil

grows the arc and tighter up
the eye turns, see

small promise
as birds go
south and north

MOTHS

therein a city's
infinite amber rooms
perpetually form
flare and fly off

those alive in
fear of night
would take this name
eternal flame

each cell's charge
a soul
gains wings heavenward.

blake saw
as much and builded
him Jerusalem

LEAVES

called sleeping
banks by the un
born wavering in
leaves and light

in leaves care light
tucks faces.

for speech, a body
and breath.
but these have only songs

to the sun!
see the round mouths hollowed
by the wind,
the silver flesh
the silver hands
released!

always a calling
(that i fail to hear
the source of
an angular descent, a coming
in blocks
a stairway
so when all signs agree
the approach
is possible
the multiple
many
one of many arms and most especially
joinings of arms openings
arrest
heart silver thread

but i am only

bound this seeing
is a light come out of me
a semen
seals to prosper
so that, that one, I love, appears
a monarch
standing and unfolding
all aspects, peaks
known to me in
and in and
where my love is
comprehended there

there

MAIZE

published by Pentagram Press
1979

as each in its time turns
leaf swimming
pierced by the sun red
sun
whose rhythms
hand to hand to hand imagination
peace leaf here trace

beauty rides an air, denies
perfection
words hard lozenge
earth swallowing
losing threads to resolution

treads to revolution
print in earth
hard step
harvest is the seed
labors end
moon whose daily passage would divide
shoulder grain and arms
equally

the moon red
moon harvest
is mine sun sower
as is the time it marks
light sliced throughout the season leached
with leaf-mulch
all my wages
revolution
return
is this identity of place
deepens to my depth
soil, clay and rock
bed

as flint strikes to spark
many feet
glance a hardened earth
the dance all flesh and gesture given
seeks community
that plot
known and known.
as dancers limb-spun sashes
fan to celebrate
sunset

each fingering probe toward night
a name of light
color
fully felt without filling
eye
cup of love
made by light that we may

fall leaves representative
hands that pass from the mind
color, gesture, symbol, tongue, speech
leaf falls here
forms a language
of us

TRIO

of the Approaching Life

published in Samizdat
1980

untaken you
pierce
a thought's bright bole

and mad-armed
cut
from one child yet another
stillborn

that most don't pass
knive stile

who speaks
say one is uncreated
voice before fire

uncreate
earth upon matter the weak and dead
your limbs bent by the plea
turn

praise God
blade in the moving
water

bearing God divided
stone from stone

name

before foul orifice the flame   where name is not
falters

(retreat to dream
you
maiden the mind
speak in me i fear
to utter erases

that in me i may
the dark, the formless
logic concede
to love come wounded

intoned body
pool shape of bell
without sound amplifying   word before word
in ear, tongue
instrument

intimate liquid, spread who   of combining and diffracting

of poet
know me out of me

pushing waking through
inversion
array
by desire

at teeth collect and
attend vapor

kindly in the beast

retrace you
subtly moving

mere sheet beneath sun
prepare
for image blind us

arrive on wave
full-lipped, weighted curve
of instep, ankle, thigh, socket

fold in wing wrap
alar density
unite

axis
turn in earth's magnetic arms
collecting prey
web mind

kill and kill
that as light burst distant
cloud trembling

orbit
situate grace

cultivate the mad
step allow smaller
step shadow

lies beauty
doubting

i through that
afflicted eye
eclipses

emerge image
inverted
sun on paper
comprehend
ray

raise song
i wind curl in hollows
note us, wing
split air
come rest in song

come to comfort
face all feminine faces
flickering lamp

distant

you reign over animals
run before storm
lance

your presence
among mountains

your anger above us,
cutting wheel, strikes
and laughter

and heal again
blood song

divine the heart exposed
through wound
unheal form tender labia
of breast
ever child
leap true word

glory be
to the host, child
of all blood
bear river of blood
thrill
that all life
issues

fold unifold
angels plate strike
thunder
of your contours
thew and reverent gesture given
arms against rest

(tide's worry,
blending song
recede

come form
star risen in the east
who
of radiance reproduces radiance
sphere
sister

the children

Tamarisk Press

1981

THE CHILDREN

for Robert Creeley, Jennifer and John Taggart

the children appear and depart
and in the mind's moments

i walk with you in the dark
ways we listen to hear

one
seals the day of the other

one

an air
specific

to refine love's riddle
that this
all happens

in fear
find the thickest
progress.

fair
pressure

so keep their place
by night blossoms
one limb

from laughter

the fortunate
the inconclusive

knives

the minds'
sun
similar shadows
two of one
projects

lack of day.

say
a word,

say love.
our black steps preserved
on the burning plain
never seen

sa-rah, sa-rah, where have you been?
see here, say these violets, turning

she

framed first by the window
then only the thought

the metaphor is old, and i
retire my plan

identical quantities

of her map
& mine,
the same town
so nearly similar.

this precise increment
distances
to imagine an angel

when she enters
make
but thin protest

eases
the giving
convenes

Song's what binds us, John,
I'll make one
In your wake. Proceed.

Look
into my eyes.
This same gradual fire
replacing
has its trace in the music
which consumes

all that I am stone
persisting negligence.

We
take the form
of our uncertainty.

A shared vitality
unspent
eye that startles:
I find it ever open.

A slow flame opening
with the jet.

Is you and is not you;
is and isn't

from the horror you proclaim
in possibility
winds and twists a dying
thing created
and similarly burned.

Call it the heat,
our presence in disease
and in beatitude

that draws you toward the angel of perfection

a line drawn thinly
to define a plane
of particular resonance.

A greenest line seeks circular
fulfillment,
in the srystal holds
tones elevations,
and pure concentrated movement
is the science
of its release

as mouth frames uttering O,
as eye must be a sphere
organizing light

I say
the word love
knowing the word
fails

that all parts meet
in time's considerate structure,
bare graph of lines.

You stand struggling
in our light

trees budding even in darkness
over us
to listen in their way
what currents come

and I am the body of this moment
listening.

Poems

from Origin 20 (ed. Cid Corman)

July 1982

GRATITUDE

for Dr. Allen Ott

come
through
light's attachment
the figure
stands
behind
the figure

layers of movement
in each thing knotting
to an eye
wherever mine

desire to leave
light
isolate

waiting within
sensation

a wave awkwardly
moving among sea
grasses,
on sand

little one
escaping
the cold halo

entering
the primitive
corridor

in conflict,
sacrifice
permits thoughts'
others,

woods
stone
grasses,
change
in exclusion

held at my
perimeter

that is the force of my
desire

sun
weaving of branches
the larger body

that is

what the sun has woven
shades

in a field collecting
reason

out into the small
curls
of a leaf

growing
dark

thoughts beneath procession
beneath clouds
aging

where winds barely ran
patterns
pass informing
a plain of wheat

to nothing
having given it all
away

inamorate moon
night's signs
flare and dissipate

as your losses
become opaque

we sleep and wake
on earth
unaware and
unable to read
gravity

the greater
passages
listen after

within whose shape
two sounds
simultaneously generated,
meeting,
cease

lamenting
the calm

perforating
cover
song finds sticks
to make a circle

say
in seeing me
now
that day our love
gains

in you
the wood
winds audient

through the arc of the sun's
day passage

that is constant impermanent
acting two

gathering in absence
impressions of paradise

breaking the code

'the figure
stands
behind the figure'
relinquishing the burning
outline you
the one presented
indicate impassively
consumption
and its correspondent
despair the clamoring ceiling
rise into
discarding
spending
identity, the holy
fear
in stone
variously woman
self and decay
reinstate
distraction
that your work
I must accomplish,
your work
I must accomplish
in the alien earth
impress and deepen
this circle that it may
a cavern
active air in forming

from the ancient
each proceeding each more full
finding resonance
toward speech without sound
audience
always less than one
always through
pain's most horrible and quick
elation of breath
red hand
seizing blue sky
or the eye cannot confuse
the images of heaven

it is in gratitude
these words are written
a man a complex
of the between
coherence

that urgency in
hosting the   white
consumed
in crude   white
mechanical succession   white
is my only
son and parasite   acts
companion   where walks insensible
to a poem,
gesture,   companion
all that can be seen
if the eye   with
possess its power   am undivided
and cease perpetually
rules me, fire   simultaneous
or vernal death
given ear given access   stays
studded agent   cell-rigid
who in acquisition   culminating the image
recognizes theft   no longer engaging
and menacing of aspect roils   means capacity
against the senses
emptied
few held to drink   oval
seize in hesitation
deafness   of sounds
the threshold and the name   thorn
there written   of rumbling
chosen and neglected   a clap

the indistinguishable	extinguishes
gift and humility	
diminished	here for silence
	the chain
that is a posture	laughs also
track obscurity, false	
cradle of two	leaving
for one star	effects
object object believing	discarded
more or less	
the adumbrated outer	taken in the eye
harbor of ill wind seen	conditional
stalking,	upon birth agreeing
strategy to show love	ignorance
will assassin	to show love
waits as if the infusion	
the rule of parts	elegiac walk
adheres	that it does not
at the shore, dry sand,	materialize
hesistant	
	hymn
glory waste another shell	or the spheres
facing its beyond-attainment sweet	burn
lie	refused
in involuted settlement	accord with experience
clothed argument	to penetrate
reflects	
	continues
of the walk, of parts	death

from their describing colloquy	unnecessary
estranged, the child	but the ear
chose tree, flower, stream	
for thirst	that has atrophied
three times denied	not of
	hearing
to mineral as the imprint	speech secondarily
seeks record	dispersal
find all terms applied	
recessive, loved	locates
cleft loam from loess deny	character
on climate	failing
which of her body dreaming	divorce
sways intact	
	in obverse
perishable	resource
crooked stick enamoured of sense	virgin
to a third, more violent	valley and hill
piety lament	repose
	a vocabulary
no more than a shuddering takes	vented
the accessory observe	essence
blunt pain through disaffection	
that to wandering consigns	steps
the beautiful dumb in fire	over
lost to wishes	their movement
dark in day	assesses
the inventor	a logic
corner animal in	of under

graced
tense symmetrical   by independent
horror comes inevitably to act   fallen
erase the moment, art   to impress
serves none without life

spring to the question, bathe   accepting
in flame   the returning
the question   feature
facing
dove call in solitary wood   immobile
or vision of drowning take   simultaneous
self-conceit from slate leave   point
fossil dwelling I   of attachment
succumb not to the event   given
but to the source   expression
of resistance   peace
I've denied   in love
cultivated
detail looks
through
integrated
much
the part
one
of

series/bond

series

bond

strife
suppose a name.

initiation and transmission
in the simple objects of a
book defining

author, captive
strife
a sum concealed
believing

that corner
itself passed, and passed
inordinate affection

scales the wind
scatters rot.

reading these, their ignorance
in configuration, a high

warning
blush
the stone

night's element among them,
expressed as it appears
of the pain
precedent,
steps

the unifying
conversant

behind
the call

reports
at the threshold sways

the stem
on which
she rested.

"come,"
forward
the water
no longer owns

READING

for Doug Messerli

a reflection of hands
that wavers
up the street with
suppressed

the interruption
between us
time

of year when transport,
the thin shoots to
lapses
to wake
on the ground with leaves
gone from it,
two

as two at once, but from
oneself curiously

performing.
fingers
and the other
spectator
dress the daughter
stands
and fills.

II

the new green to erase itself
in the story of light

inflating and diffusing
wishes to condemn the imagined
to have been there before
arousal, leaf,

in and away torment
spring, wrench
the parent, signature.

you
stand
in that near
could
receive

a partial childhood, one
from many the opaque
riddles decline

our season.

III

resisting
the slope

whatever is to hand
unravels.

SYMBIOSIS

for Sue Horvitz

arc	
to	
learn	from
weighs	the beginning
silence	rods
binds	smoothly
	moving
	in and out,
	the facsimile,
	deeply
the room	felt
asks	
be consumed	renewed
its	sun
six identities	of a mystery
	to eyes
implicit in	unused
waking	tin
repress	and wood
dreams	congregate
walking	
near	one
giddy with it,	of-a-kind
	without value

the processional
object
no object,
greater
than the eye's   loves
compass   objects
extending
conceding,   love
cup   over obdurate
eclipses   rush
cup,   blood
and in the shadow   severance
extols
light
rusts
the inscription

THE YELLOW FLOOR

starlings
escape   utterance
in sensation
gesture's   duplicates
pure   flight
means
accumulate   children of
the vertical   dialog,
the plane
variously
at departure   open
joining

trace
extremities

Ladder

Loot 3:2 (a supplement to *Spectacular Diseases* Magazine)

July 1983

The first poem in which I recognized the representational value of a multiple-voiced text was *Ladder*. Written on learning of my friend's death, a serial transformation was to provide for her ascent. Harmonics at intervalent passages could be distinguised from the dialogue of names, and I worked, in successive poems, on extending the evolution of a resulting metaphor. The composer John Campbell encouraged me in this, at times even performing experimental works with me. We also struggled with collaboration in writing, which led to the poem *Secrets*, requested by John and later scored by him for boys' choir.

The two critical terms which have served in these works are suspension and extension. It is an architectural suspension, that a form consciously chosen and executed can suspend apparition, and provide an insular location for resumption and return. "that urgency…" would be the most "theoretical" of the poems here presented, that its extension, in light of the horror of its subject matter, was possible, for me, only in the climate of hope permitted in the dialogic suspension. What is real in this is the continuation of sound beyond the cessation of the exchange.

Gil Ott 1981

LADDER

(dreams of holly maddux)

(a poem for two voices)

Constant light phenomenon
never asked it is written we

one jewel
speak
but do not understand

after jewel, girasol
sun borne on wheels
serve blind, blind, narrow the road
vowel, our name is entrance

vocal, turning on turning, torque
torment from her banded neck a circuit
never seen complete, a guess
tergiversate, circle of jewels
                circle of stars, two eyes
versing, sun and moon closing
in
turn on uncoil the road makes road
hardened light in pieces strung

between
we take on accident
things seamless open
to our touch
petal vortex bud of light
and travel
all degrees we carry her
the way lost

an unsure progress and
a door
step's weight heard, a
time,
eternity cuneate in her
gown's foliage

grown to a seed in time
closing
our parallels diverge

all trees
say cause without eyes i wake

bitter wedge crimps sex
from umbrage

breeds moments

alphabet, degrees of her

the way lost

sigh

sough under wine hipped
soil

falling
seeds foment first early
death
divides me several in storm
seen
scatter light
am many

one jewel
transparent cube
facial cube transparent

converge
passing — fast in gravity my bowed strings
we pass on — hold fast the dark wood arches
bend arrow to use, torn melody
unite
all rays

resolve to moon, leaves
hide me from that light,
dance nether self, tide ark
silent clock

say
cause quivering shafts i wake
a tree

alert light's trace alive
startles
full to the tips, rings, diadem,
diaphanous sleeves display leaves' harmony
drawing words in spires
filling i free this oval

owed to clarity ovate
in sips it face
faces overture within eyes visage   incipient case, i usage
genitive interface   relieve

whose kin from ideal entity transpire
through skin without color

poverty tress water and bread
trace flow without movement, sound unheard,
eat us, wing
librate word say cause
the walls fall, radiant embrace

liberating
emitting
giving undepleted
rhyming
departing
filling

sky filled with eyes undiminished?
words proliferate incapable of sound?
body rising from the stream?

so the books decay,
so keen the illuminated
present.

Blue Bell,
July 1979

"SECRETS"

for John Campbell

sphere	Shore in light in darkness
	animated me, crawled beneath the seam
warm	where guardian bells disssolved
face	I hear her humming.
mother	
	Sorrow in seeing her this way, the source
moving	merely lovely, moving apart.
weakness	
	(I feel in my tendons
	sharp alien power I'd
	keep from her.)
divide	
face	And by design apply a secret magic
from	to an image garnered in the forest
face	of possible owls, of flight
a spell	and freedom, making of myself
born	two: the one
twin	who stands here in the sun, and one
	without shadow, dark, with deer
false	swiftly running and concealed.
and true	
	To leave the pale one, leave
find	the living one, discard care
strength	for the sure purchase of foot on stone,
beyond	knee's ability, strength of thigh

fear	drawn taut, the string released,
in	the shaft of air will vibrate
self	toward some forbidden heart.
climbing	
	(Eye in a bed of moss
	penetrate, send
	a messenger in flame.)
wolf	I am watched,
bear	I am instructed:
pact	the faces in the leaves approve
sworn	my nakedness and I am led
	on a dance through hunger, driven
blood	at point, to let blood.
my	
spiral	And with the sound of bees surrounding
	spiral up among blue animal spirits
all	passing out of life, thrilling
voices	surface of the waters, I
raise	descend
one	to drink
silence	to see myself.
bell	
	(Eye in the earth: a well,
	a single tone pronounces
	a single name.)

remembering	
I	Potentially a man beneath whose feet
succumb	a smaller brother, swelling vessel, pulses
	and surpasses
remembering	and leaves all portent between the two.
I	
return	How step with guidance, among
	mute sticks and matter, loss.

Alone, I build a maze
of my decisions, a way home
that accretes to me in bone, and cuts,
and closes me from ways
I'll always walk.

(In light in darkness
racing from me,
her eyes.)

January 1981

For the Salamander

Slash & Burn Press

1985

This book is for Ellen.

SALAMANDER

allowed
that would dissolve in rain
coming in and out
the many

selves presented
to the astonished
would
a color choose

and washed
sing in the hollow
under a leaf
succession

the men
step through
white to the one
and to the other

period we do not know
today
out of need
with water.

song

a
vibrates

to this moment set apart
and waiting, waves
reminded

where he wanted to go.

underbrush

deer
to my insisting
monotony

can hear you
crying

close
and
for the years
cannot

tirelessly
chosen a view

above
the isolated
meeting

all that is
overheard.

indented

hip,
shoulder,
never to speak

but fit
the theme of
all poetry

enact
in these warm cups

to the furniture
offered.

clay

hands
tensions

sense
the inviolable

matter.
metaphor

thin
as

the laboring hands
withdraw

stone

how
you need to be handled

and to my touch

respond
in what is given
of coincidence
to memory

comes
and stays
alone

photograph

the lines
bear and redeem

at
sleeping site

or waking,
I see you there

after a nap
younger

orange

traveling

apart

how much of you
I have
with

care
for the body

before any other
love
that allows
me to
with

another
section of the orange
separates and
yields.

poem

for need
nor clarity
I am silent in the hour

of conversion.
pursuit
has brought me
by minutes
this time successively
more opaque

to our accord
tied

formative
questions
in the
gaiety

which in widening
circles
includes
us

to know

sigh

fear speak of it

let
on turning in your sleep
had accumulated
to wither

the cares

silent
completed
dark of bed

to light

morning

I watched you
sleeping - only
for a moment -

your head inclined
away
from me, the dawn

of particles
composing

freedom

the hard
distinctions,

between me
and our failure

placed
the symbols

I can carefully
undress

evening

before you,
reliable
disintegration,

days and days
neither in your arms
resolved

nor
are they empty.

The Yellow Floor

Poems 1978-1983

Sun & Moon Press

1987

PRAYER

were there need to mourn
the call
dove secreted among bare trunks
would issue

word
dove intelligent nest
seen silhouette branch before space
need risen
without

sound
bird would be winged
changing
makes no sound
passing

through us

FAIRHILL

A bird—
of any family,
small and bright—
rises
startled
from a cattail thicket

wide and wide,
the freeway
to the refinery and taking
in a mud-gray creek,
tribes speak
color
the self-evident over
and patient

dancing on the dark street corner
men who by their lack of grace
are reconciled
shuffle
cold millennium
through
pavement
that a weed
become domesticated corn

ceremony
forgotten
to the city
with insignificant return

is of this furnace
a lace of bad soil,
and to suffer in work,
if given sight
to see it,
making
eating

TWO LINKED SONGS

for Cid Corman

That that that.
Sail, plume,
what gathering of atoms
must be done.

We are not sacrificed.
We are not idle.
Let the device
destroy us.

The immutable
cold to the small bones
of the face,
dark consonant rider,
past the eternal
crowing, ice
up at hips,
lastly a man.

The cape and spur. Whose
rib in the thin of, thin
camaraderie, what
pose the clot takes

for silver.
Pace, pace, nervous,
for payment.

We
walk
as one
falcon
heart
of falcon
with high
winds
commuting,

cresting,

singly
one
the strand
along:

sheer
cliffs
the continent
keep,
'the level
ocean
laughs'

scarred
carcass

without legs
rigor
more this tacit
defiance

times
mute spasms
between the echoes
of a scream.

Weight
horse
white
body
‘s troubles subsumed
in equinoctial
tide.

Far white wavering
egret
on stiff legs
dips
beak to tidepool,
to opposite image.

Fine matter
living in a live green
wash of another’s
hunger.

BLUE AT DUSK

blue at dusk, and deep
as liquid, snows
I've watched accumulate
all day

hear the call of a child's
game, the circle
does not break

peering
into
the descending
night.

Come in, the night
stripped from us, all
that in a spark is blown
beyond proportion dead, red

indefinite trouble, tie
down those already secure, friend,
through whose imagining hand
we see no longer.

More than the thought, no element
to dye the way one
evening tells me of it
or escapes the forehead, mouth

burned into a liquid we find
through being us. The putting
together of parts, artifice,
the trace we've escaped

leaving the warmth you reinforce
in a word your love. Pass
through the fire in a succession
of flames, all intimate scenes.

She thinks of
sleeping
in the early afternoon

a large and menacing
bird the dream

in a sunbeam
like a broad knife
carries.

MORNING GLORIES

How include
the leap through

that I write
and have before you

she
who came to mind,
no more

what I want to hold
impeding
arms' and eyes'
contractions

on these arranged,
the imaginary
weight.

RAIN

of talking:
the act and what
is talked about

in the immediate, tree
fed of women and men,
antedating

commerce, by commerce
the compact given to doubt,
like the rest of us

animal, discrete.
all
of water,

shivering.
a hymn in the seed
thrown

under branches
the chirping
birds.

Now, I
in the light of
others in her name
the insubstantial
images

put off
that entry
years and suffering brought
quick to resonate
this

heart's a machine
doubled with her work
in the earth
no attitude
walks.

at noon where the rabbit
slept at night
or prehistoric hunters
ringed a fire.
What same essence
turns you
from your fellow's eyes?
(Ja-da,
ja-da,
deaf-mute dances in the square,
brown wave roll up against white,
dear vision's trace
I'll take
Into hiding.)

Sea weed.
Parchment.
'the aim of an order
that might perhaps
be communicated
to all men.'
What's ordered, stave:
a rush, suspend
gestural hand,
lip pause without wind.

My friend hears.
We have no need

of conversation;
the scaling down,
the dust in place,
incomprehensible,
the labor.

INVERSION

the difference
shadow

completes
an acquisition
shell to tender
spreads

not freely given

night

a long walk

self.

the new place
strange, it borrows
from the old.

friends
and
enemy
throughout the cold
steps
report.

THE WAR

Our smallness
factors in the cold and not
by opposition detonated
bodies of men, the prophetic
wing we'll rise on,
who, men no less than we,
hold fire.
It is our smallness
frames criminal use
in the world, a world,
no world by famine trails
at random where the heat
speaks.
Small angelic accomplice
lost to night, fuse
an engine's power to your threat
that we
remain divided.

Reduced
to the sun at noon
that steeple mechanism Bach

we wanted
a companionship,
equating solitude with labor,
the movements

of a beetle
who builds and in it
believes

himself the instrument
An equivocal music, refined
to fit the hand,

soft exhalation
for the ear, on the other
end fire, perfectly made
cautionary science of it own end

in a mob, one
of the others
trampled

matrix of feet.
At the controls
and absent

victim
the daughters
extend no hand,
who themselves for centuries

molting:
gold
oil
radium

metropolis in ideal
stricture, the waters
and forest lacteal

borders of achievement.
Radio, synthetic
drop come through a sumac's
vein

burns on the burned
arms of the man responsible
surrendered, meek

music in his head.
Beauty in rain
a way to die
small

climb up this rock, hand
on a vine
dark
earth rips and stings a moment

on target.
Child trajectory, degrees
from rest rears

and thunders, strange
kin to alchemy
dammed

and wired
turns
the little mind

no longer a boat:
a model strung
binary, unit of resistance
mesh

cap a man
to believe and act.
Weight contact
to the required tap

or glance,
kill rather than speak,
intimate

distance.
Push you down
stairs, climb

over an old man gasping, hand
on the railing
bright
shards of the wall

bleed when touched. Nothing
doing. Between deed
and the knowing
actor, speed

turn his fault,
machine his image
inert and unsubmissive, calibrate

it like us,
let it run,
be patient.

CEREMONY

own making

the time, a thin and
prudent to the objects on the table,
the disorganized proximate
making of me

waiting
for you, but for any
settling

within the cup, leaves
in paper.

Public Domain

Potes & Poets
Elmwood, CT

1989

I am calling forth a poem.
I am calling forth a poem.

Come help me sing the song.
Come be with me the poem.

In darkn

When your eyes
to gain's distracting
blur the fearful
pull of your mate past ease

strain on the road hope
that place your mind only
accommodates hemorrhage

sweet to the edge or ignorance
potent *dulce*
grips the wheel, to yourself
reddening

may ask the cause
of your trouble

within the germ
a tear, strange to you and past
your thin
nerve driven.

INTRODUCTORY

Language accretes, and molds itself around the precipitant moments of a culture. Where there is cause for celebration, it emerges specific, even ritualized. Where doubt or shame, it covers up and reproduces rapidly, scrambling for the right terms, on to its own complicity.

Poets are born into an acute awareness of these facts. In the United States, our relation to the dominant culture is defined by production of – or our abstention and criticism of – contributory linguistic ornament. The activist role is discouraged for the poet, and it has, today, in the US, atrophied.

Where poetry is permitted to lead, it heals. The poetic processes of attentiveness, association, and performance, overlay essential mental, emotional, and bodily functions.

But the poet's alienation is severe in those societies where the processes of language are cloned and the clones promoted by controlling institutions to rationalize or conceal racism and genocide, or to cheat working men and women. It is a primary task of the poet to question and, as times demand, to challenge such authority. Working men and women are, after all, the majority consumers of language, insatiably so when we are denied our complementary creative, language-making role.

Fortunately, we are not often jailed for our poetry alone in the US, though we *are* jailed for our activism, that is, for our eloquence. Control over the interpretation of language characterizes the true sources of commercial, religious, military, and legal power. Until each new linguistic meaning and form is catalogued and cast as artifact by someone in this crowd, the respect it receives alternates with the suspicion it raises. And America has shown its willingness to act against the writer whose work remains a threat.

Tutored on a consumerist model, those writers in the current American literary community who sense their own failings are offered security in the essentially economic formula: profession = marketable commodity. Personal style, association, and theoretical dogma figure as the professional writer's capital, and accommodate this retreat. Of course, it is to the literary community's credit that it shelters the articulate victims and refugees from the debacle. Yet in America and Europe, the literary community as a whole makes up a class, and it does harbor charlatans.

Language is no one's. Never was. The true site of all language is in the pairing, writer to reader, speaker to listener. The poem is public event, host to a multitude of private entries, a defined anarchy. Understood and practiced in this way, it is powerful.

The regimentation of meaning is criminal, even in the least increment. Language is at once ambiguous and persuasive enough to offer itself as a tool to advantage and oppression, and seen as medium, neutral. Complicity in this crime, as auditor/actors as much as speakers, contributes heartily to our public experience and behavior, as consumers, workers, citizens.

The poems in *Public Domain* are antipathetic to such complicity. They should be spoken aloud, and they should be heard. Look for their author on the street, driving or walking to work, thoroughly exposed. Look to yourself.

LEVELS ADDRESS

Why start with a self-reflexive question? The imperative levels address. What I have needed, simply to get off, is that illusion of form address implies. The bi- or multi-polar, talking to.

One hour from now is waiting. What anxiety inheres, wants out, to bud. So much behavior, between us, fixes our suspicions. But I have tools to make an index.

I am satisfied with very little. Dusk begins my day and continues in lengths, undifferentiated. Write neither of, nor substitute, to keep you, reading. After all, honesty is only custom, or better, custom is custom. Each full page waits against argument, then, taken from neglect, asks questions.

Watch what falls from this tree. Step up, and shake. Name's
____________________. Was that mine? Come closer.

Observe, speak. Inequivalent in method, but essentially questions. Always letting one out, then sorting fish. What is the gesture for breadth of acceptance? Once you start interpreting things, it's hard to stop, and who's to say you should? A man arrives with a big white sheet; the ice gets thicker. Think of you think of yourself.

What current language is available to us all, a gloss and pitch, more than its freight determines commonality.

How many are you? I write a letter to the one I love best. Some write back, but never really does. Love wasn't the idea.

Finding the time for many receipt, as, consolidating many to one, times harden. That is difficult. Compose, be calm. Theft takes a steady hand, and patience. How many are you, hear me?

Never minding what's said, is intransitive implies you. Take my advice. Questions, toasts, confessions, suggestions… lead. To me. Look at it from my point of view. From consensus hums like a house, or other pleasant-sounding logic, always plain. Get by the neck and think it.

Remember my days in what show fluid. I anticipate yours, suggest a beat. Look at yourself. An agreement we rewrite. My currency in yours, grace.

> We are concerned
> each
> with you on your flight
> art accustomed to one moment
> only me. That you have committed

act independently,
redundantly to yourself.

Strength
a prayer work fecundate
alone, a footprint, two
won't hear. We send
slip into an envelope conceived
outside our text's
necessary reference.

Lord, speak
these difficult
in our hands fragments value
that you will commit, to raise
child, precursor.
Small faith
take.

He'd left her a note, tomorrow.

Chance precedes a shudder, which pops on before dawn. Venus, weak by comparison, is drowned in the difficulty. Light in his eyes, blinding him, hubby piled up his rig, tied up the highway. Past harbors, harbors examples. Without means, the shudder keeps running. She snaps the lead.

"The problem with him
insistence, with no need to answer any questions. Persons unnecessary, address diffuses. I can report to you that he. Started in mid-step, he ran. We might erect a fence, or just suggest limits, arbiter. Either way without a doubt.

You'd by what I call necessity, by what's inherent. I want to go back from the light in my eyes. I might make it a narrative's already done. The project

Talking around
that's hungry at the site of me. A rich foam satisfies my inhabitant. Today, to buy a chance on tomorrow. Talk of origins; talk of names. Equal mine ever, like I'd bought the goods he calims he never offered.

In on it's complicitous, gnawing inside. Am rhetoric could kill the speaker, taste of blood like copper. Ate my fingertips. Greed, the object, 's words untutored from a mouth. Sick. Knocked out a tooth.

But let's get next to each other. Call me by my first name. What's your pleasure? Are you comfortable here? Will you need me for anything else

(having
left
a question
in the odor of gas

my
heart accelerated
down my

wanted relation
to a substance
worm

can't
turn you loose. Anybody's guess assumed a map of alien terrain. Willing, but stupid, the spirit, to. Filled my throat. Knob off in my hand the door swung open, and I shoved reflection to a holding. What choice? These days I liked to raise the image of my obsession to an in on party. He has his own intentions. No room for the infirm in agreed behavior.

A part of net when isolated, otherwise taken out of love. But into electric, then unwind. Stay clean. Transgress. This competitor is mine; hold him, it, in me. The parapet diminishes, I think, then stepping over it, wake to pain.

Ignoring the world in me. Male to persevere, an enemy in gestate overcome. I'm bored through the wall, violated, by a language making so much fucking sense to me. Conceived in heat, which suckers thrive in a loaf, in a basket? Attack 'em pell meel, they divide your efforts. What drum at a maggot.

The freedoms
of the addict
comforts
what
I'm talking about into
any skull whatsoever
its own fever
to a row of palms by fire from behind the conflict
lit adolescent glory, a chosen,
a long drive chewed through dominance.

Host to refinement needing definition in blood let
strapped a foregone mix to dispel pain. Introduce
a toxin seals the solution keeper kept
off an acre's capability, its requirements
exhaust the hostage.

The struggle in blue, for allopathy, narrative holding out for dawn. Upped the ante plays it big on opposing flanks, all bulk without detail. Anthem through a powder hole to your own thoughts, if you've got any.

Care for a knot

bled tissue vales to call a domicile, mistaking
aperture's phase. Tending kin

    to my old
    muck
    the willed
    arrest
    damned
    exhalation
    mirrors

YELLOW FIELD

for analogue
sets a comma
to planed wood

marking a
you for my
periodicity

burns, and how it
wrecks me
revives me

gone to the furthest
outpost, grain
to take a name

wed
alcohol to wood the chalice
broken

force
detected
damned initial

like a blade flies
to disregard
tenders demise

'd mirror & mirror
constituting
stands a place

atop an image, music
pressed from several
sides

with me returning
means distinct
contention

gloved
at birth or birth
assuming eminence

on histories
exaction
tax transgress

a pinprick in a poem
bring
that brick down

LONG

Each evening's banked
clouds at an altitude to drive

the question home. No counting what
brings torpor on. Models topple

unresolved and the road not taken, taken,
stinks. Salmon on blue, she's stretched

before her invitation fails in headlights
or a head throb, doting on minutiae

in the way of my dust. The pronouns
deceive, been legion, but my practical

testing middle age demands one even
as rules go to play. Take her,

for instance, trussed but ambiguous figure
of speech, a mental image eager

to serve. Think of it and roam,
swerve. Eyes on the road.

WHITES

to tell it
calm and quietly
starved of my
owner

habit to gloss, tossing her hair. Wants blocking wants her woolen pleats, her silk. Grace among needs to impoverish. Look! A draw that know myself awkward and premature.

Declined's active, rejected passive. Hop a slot where people live like roaches. Choices of sexual idiom tack me to another post. But each has his use. Squeam a little here, a little there, soon everyone knows you. And you are abundant, available

to the market for albums, magazines, tobacco and alcohol. She's no fade. A pastime of suffocate clears dreams of seductions, leaves soot. Cherry, Cherry, out all night, shopping.

Too many matinee idols pile my lost opportunities in the sink. Later never comes. Out that window, in the field behind the house, further, bought

tickets to vicarious
battery
vents captain's
pent anger

dulled by conflict. Hunger obeys. Want a blow job? The servant dips and scram enforced nightly. Customs flourish at the *bal du siecle*, ringed by caliber. Ladies and soldiers remain loyal to form. There within the out

back a nuts jungle piously spreads his legs. He applies the iron. That sack of bones is closer to the Lord than I. God sort 'em out. Buffalo nickel, Indian head penny, tender wood limb acquiesces, turned their propaganda on themselves.

Abraham came out of the tall grass, pale from fervor. He gave the workers the day off, and sat there by himself. He'd had a vision of the future (this is not one of his more famous exploits), determinist linkage and auto-trans, damning, never doubting himself. Were ovens

affecting little
bait to jail

stamina, limited, furious. Expect to bulge, dye in the carotid artery. White knuckles, Rolls of whites edged the woods. I'm going in under cover. The treaties are a crock of shit. My cattle were took, and mine's downriver to heathen. I'll need help.

Combustion engines outside, electric motors in. Bits of powder bits crosses an information line otherwise numb. Keeps progressives on their toes. Rude to organize suicide you

capacity
to turn them
erotic
conflict

Went up her moving image. I saw to it twice, until it left. Some distributor's desire to exploit saturation to a tissue. He wants a buck. He minds his business.

Serially fixate broke off at the turn in the road, onto a convenient billboard, but spilled as well, sinking in. Sneaked a chocolate. Ha ha! You're home early!

congruence and plenitude

remember who I am at any moment. Resisting returning. On a shelf in the second of those rooms, something I've made rests. Paper and clay uncertainly. Now I want to test the man on the phone, at the counter, my desk. You and I listening hear the similarity. Multiply

the determinant
act preceding insight, from that dark gradually
your face, and then, as if into myself

repeatedly and without distinction.

Talking about the violence in the act, how plain expression accumulates a code. I want to touch and you, to be absent. The pauses, countenance, become perfect alum. The pauses

privileged to talk about loving you. The rest of the language is out on strike. Who will replace the woman never correctly thought? The question is wrong, but one of intention. At what point has she retreated?

Strange to judge a man, dancing with him. Too loud to talk keeps them from me. We need this formality for practice, simulating in the mood. I like to keep my thoughts short.

I asked him when the machine would be free, the whole day so a month or year, a coin in my mouth. He's at the controls, profile, full view, identifiable. I hate the model to the real thing, who's just turned away again.

sex of the air, my
hips
mind behavior alone among books
fine
to achieve notoriety
set
that tree to that rectangular
heat

pays on receipt
keeps his thoughts to himself. Remember the guy in the red suit? Down payment is a disease like any other. A habit. Keep your eyes on street level, off folk, there's goods

occupy affection. So shoot me. There's no law says I can't

impersonate

fellow professionals. Pornography in the age of mechanical reproduction. Reproduction itself. Hip to axle, spoke of water rising to a well. The skin like a rubber tarp, pulled over it, wave register.

When
symmetry in two lines
and a gap between

enough
past into myself waiting
for him at the door

omit my black
skirt, the look she never

business
done in there.

itch at watch
against a corner

stockings midthigh
to the hem

wormed
leather

case lightly in his right hand. Shoes as thin transmit the stone's texture. Linoleum stings. Under his arm the forty-seven postures boxed estimably. "As if heat had to be invented!" he laughed, at tomorrow's meeting

pulled his chain. The girl is not pretty. Address the men, one woman in suits, as arranged. Beat the hell of a tight sock

sober to bruise
were no more children
to garter

nailed or pierced the little web abandoned, and he flushed. He wept. Temperate pressure a balls corona, the blood pushed back and pushing back. Bonded

aggress waiting for the light to change. Clock her neck from the street upstairs to strap and ride, appointments waiting.

lost another year
that pads the girl
up, down, in and out of view
toughs it, ignorant, took one around the corner
in some
doorway.

place violated by an early dusk
trusted what device a man installed
against enduring,
the hard breath up at noon
's boiler to accompany me
to bed at any premium.

smell th' polyurethane's aged and brittle
past weight, light out under my scalp as I go
down, fume and trash
on entry only only answers myself
talking
followed me home.

lost
footing a mouse's shadow followed
th' exact curve, a man no bigger out
my side wriggles and tugs brown liquid
crenellate the stub's remaining
vengeance, resists.

small threats under appurtenances mine, draw kinship
out multiplying signs, actual voices out
of synch
spun, drop, accelerating, pierce one

unremarkably, with this fist opening and any
grit mixing

as unified.
A house's cat's sniff about shit congeals it.
Keep else's fears to reading, Hand,
attend and recognize these
leaves fallen
on no dead.

YELLOW FIELD

notion of driving
head, or slats
to a wall

that overlay as over
vapor
of the fur

torn in an eye
from cover
came an accusation

she'd
me darkly
whisper

past a mat prohibited
descent
grasses

hatched, divided
talling over
dirt

from angels indiscriminately
spread
a figure, copula

illuminate
a gesture
will without

you
privately
blood

transgress
along a fir branch
quivers

drops
as dropped
into complexity

the subject
liquid
seeping

wound may be too great to finish telling. No source to it, the illness moves. Every object blank when I am looking in my mind among injuries. The poem to think. Better of coincidence of a sensory world shunned the acid.

The red out of the cat's mouth proud you a sucker to your face. Hit his hat hatchet job on you've worked for, despair of. Class of violence wants the very rocks off that hill. Chase him down a crease, onto the street and under a truck. Under and gone.

Alive tolerate the equivalence of your pain. The Miskito in the way, the Mayan, in Salvador, Atitlan, you've done for playing along. The price you pay or get out.

I've made terms on put the hemo, coil in solution up-my-sleeve wheeled to a poorer neighborhood. A chorus of hard comparison. Out every brick vault grew disoriented to took ambulatory, sharded out, away from me, out.

My hand more than my eye, as it passes over that primitive, coded
pattern, more of soil

streets we knew

walk with you.

The stores and houses in a regular grid are more than silent, and meet their excess with a silence

in need of any verse agreed tacitly to imbue. Its fabric, like a map, needed us, or, later, me alone, and tolerated my control. Memory's the ruse. Present value translates not into labor but that theft

glass from sand to condemn

abstract. This money represents an

paradox revealed only in the loss. I see a weft to the line of poplars. Your house is on the right.

This is the way a dream dispels pain. It, too, draws from a store

out there alone. A material simulation says the same thing. Or a new friend. The heart mismanages

tactile share. The garment's scarcity means both poverty and wealth, we attribute to its makers. That you carried that cloth equal to the translation

it lost what I had already denied you.

She listens to the radio while busily tones her flesh. Hum time of day, of industry, as every day her movements brush her nipples on her shirt, she bends to sweep. Were there sudden rain it wouldn't fill more space. Dark atmosphere and light, warm and chill contending. Unique, proudly at work con densing the countertop.

The defensive stance has the worries the vehicle, who only a moment ago thought herself a machine. Spite is possible to be happy, grinding it out. Vulnerable to cheer concedes from in or out a muscle, or a muscle system resolve to count coin. Push a thigh, bowels, nausea.

She hasn't tired of syntax, driving, or what's to come. Make it up, and add to this addictions defrays late clarity. Surround ed by disorder needs a blood gluepot, touches herself, near winged. Pauses. Continually the plains, the preparations meet, surround, subdued, pass into memory that is, for all her elasticity, a window elsewhere.

Twelve lanes compress to six behind the row of houses opposite.

Blood pooled in her calves, her thighs and back when her fertile button popped. Voices through the wall, the girls next door, a cried in a rented room. What's re-sidual, the walls confused? Heavy stiffened. Then she turned and brushed his buttocks through the covers, intentioned and unreasoned.

Her step on that loose floor board wakes him.

Night everywhere but here. I come in to counteract discomfort. The eyeball for bloodshot, finding it, ashamed. Choose retreat over quizzy, Jack's accident scene. His phallus, this body. In a noise grate sends me wander lonely, to me, myself. Stores on stores, and clouds above a silhouette dad talks mom away. Be be be baby. Came potted meat weight, of the arms hung from clavicle, spine to mat, for freedom. Dad to momma tap tap tappa tap tappa tap – I'm dancin'! Till fatigue and otherwise cool, ambiguous groin. Thus fertile. A primer little more than no explanation.

She to all women I to she. Plane to wood a square of moonlight taut: a logic. Twelve interior edges, but to one the palindrome to me hushed.

Who put the bolt spins from her far galaxy. How her body knows so little save when toddled trusts her own devices. Has learned today osteo-isolate to break a posture, to change tomorrow. The several means to accede, spread a mat, to split. Slumps.

The glass moves a pinpoint familiar to a field out of spin.

"Of her weight, although she didn't physically lean on me. I'm at the machine, typing, and she's standing behind me. Make me nervous!"

"I'm telling you, or somebody, not my old boss in the hallway, to a rattling of peers.

"Thoughts that cut another shorten me. Came to cry, addled Becky not yet on's conspirator unwavering. Too much Latinate following no letup from the phone subdues me. Next undergrad moves up, my neck stiff, my sub on break. Tired. Tired of articulate."

Learning to cross more than filigree out to reading each day singly, a world.

Puts on, her coat. A confidence about a comment scores the marriage. Tarns of them Catholic girls count for less. Julia scolds the neighborhood, but it's a bad night's sleep, traffic to come heads her tongue. She returns to sweet on him, the vestibule turtling up with her in it still. A moment. A parting. Breeze portending rain toward her car.

Let the problem draw it close to recedes. Fits like a hat. The rupturings a more appropriate pronounced her loins in determining tides. Doubt to surer politics, braking downhill. None of it's easy. Half past last spotted.

TO JULIA'S HAND

Due to the tensile swift
at an edge dispels

around my waist, or any circle you
and I determine utterance, what's in

performer to an intimate grasp, locked
lightly

your failing fails of its disclosure.
A random confidence the apprehension

tests a gate, opposable
as ancient teeth, tongue, thumb and index
absently count. Alternating in
and out and wanting
all in the fuse reiterated, yet to injury
exposed as scarified, grip deferring

a life of service along the serrate
fin confluent to the brookside.

Expressing what's difficult
strands you've worked
or daily meet, what comic
parrots necks of a wrist

from intimacy subject to intimacy told me
quick I'd owned in sentiment only, vertebrae neatly
separated and, too full a portion, fallen.
Out of precedent, unfitting, never saw
sent on what wire, you hold my

signals, thoughtfully in check. You are cool,
a little damp, mine. From every far

accretion
palm to absolve
it tested

quietly, holding the pen.

RADICALISM

Before gone requiring a stronger vehicle. Reach pushes into the dry soil doesn't emerge. Emerge continually, you plow and dissolve true radical.

Before names passed and is standing over us in which tree, by this message, collecting bits of mineral to petrify. I'm singing to the past up there marching, brutally tricked and not to my illusions. History in telling without asylum peace in the blood, tyranny in language.

given
under sycamore. Applied it came to me like an idea. Curl in rust. I have worked and worked to this grain collectively, whose

deaths inform a stroke of filing, filings lining up. The goal: seamless effort. Keep from freezing with a song, in turn, from memory's duration

overturn deceit. Con-
flated deci-

material
from ash re-
trieved

a visible flame. Planed wood tree reassembling, so from bone,

friend, my vocabulary spreads, pales at senses. My shadow in shade. Carry
sack of others'
compositions; no

matter, they'd'a ate
your family.

Get
bit. Limp. Mix

wisdom and dirt. Don't
be too obvious

when you talk
to fish.

(... Names never wrote but laughed. Thinking, once the movement of my branches, out of text or accomplished. Difference is past here. Trace, chart a course, its source in the present that's the sound of leaves at the end of summer, clatter.)

How come to terms with a comfort volume control a visitation phantom selects? My method has gaps, ignoring me? Whose program the beginning but unending staccato conceives in ruts (a word), troughs (waves), anger (silence), and none precisely.

Parent educates veils a threat. The difficulty of starting a leg up in the grave. Settle down. Heard any jokes, the late cynic ecology continues to gnaw, better than me, than most. Processual to rot her downstairs alone in bed, watching TV. A man to answer to. A vulnerable man. A man's hand aging, twitching, etched and untrustworthy. God love the bugs are hit and flying.

Between you and me, whose perspective fits description? Tied a ribbon on that tree, there. The dye ran. Name became the name of name exaggerates to strangle lesser senses. Then damned if the mind don't start to go.

Caught rubbernecking. Transit toward a wood, first memory, without effort. To an alley offers comfort. The people near wiped-out deny myself food. Lakota, side of the highway. A leg off in the story. The irrelevant versioning possesses so much land strung out.

Either way, I've got the best microbial surface. Think about it a trilling bird sings, it's sunset! That swelling, that dream about disease subject, to take care, predicate. Fucking commas, catch my feet.

In that heat whose purpose felt the pull of muscle over bone? Hard work the body's fall wouldn't want, got took by the sun.

Up in heaven I was attested by bees bright yellow and *indifferent* to me. A friend held one foot, a rope around my neck, I took my first step. The earth would not record my weight. Past then the men broke voices in me, matter-of-fact, I wanted one or many. To this day my hips are numb, and slur my speech.

Story my decay, my life. Given to pleasure choices a swollen finger kids to its relent in stupor. Dialogical with the end predicted, a truth. Syringe cause of the trouble. Laugh at the rush in my temples, the heat engendering a spin. How political is hunger? I wrote a clue for my time tomorrow, flickering painlessly.

Accident of birth asks I seek a violent end tutored eyes on else. The lord's indifference hot potatos it from that scene, or needn't, the sanctuary built on swamps. Some serve. I drove the car into the tree, Officer. You see a dry need; I'm otherwise incapable.

Past dignity
to we who disbelieving formed a ring
the smoke shot through the grass
bellowing

in its simplicity
pure hell closed ‘round
a hole in the night.

What’s known *reposite* what cannot be mentioned. Two of me. One in the pit, ill, the other peeling leaves away.

The surf is organized, yet tired slate that works for everyone. With no thought containing the work of sleeping, conflict, which among children is a badge won out of danger. But such risk earned pushes a thought past thinking. Nausea. The loving hand familiar’s lost its blood, falls. Never done move onto something else.

attack had put him back in the hospital. The tape ran out, so I didn't get his number. Calm, Bill's face before me, difficult friend, but in the urgency I felt in dialing the hospital's main desk to get it, friendly duty. He may die, that's clear. Write it down. Thank you. Hang up. Hesitate

the same themes I'd called escapism always, and usually tried to avoid when he and I talked. The elusive teaching job in Fiji, a return to Wales, to Aberystwith, where he once taught for a year. This time I encouraged, welcomed fantasy as a real option. "I have a test on Monday. A catheter, man." Just getting home, where he was alone, lonely, cooking himself a meal, would be enough. "They put it in through my neck." Desperate sentiment. I've felt it, too, on news from the doctor. Sought more distant return. "Whatever they tell you, Bill. It's not the life

choses
safely right of the line a forward
collapse, another display, a more real
bid for succor. Transient
ends to gobble
how many more of you?
One year, four years, eight, your
dependency spent, love sotted with talk
around next
spring pushing daisies through this old overcoat. The bass line, too, disintegrated;
last bird out of the cave blinds the impatient

to paining's habit deduct regular narrowing fix on one, desired, each accursed

in writing her down. In negate. In difficulty short years sunk into dirt. We'd dug
two pits, much larger than needed, and packed. We've taken poison. A gravity
toward I've come into the narrative late. I'm with poison me.

transparence
leaves "like a shower of coins
to move among
communing, to depend

or gain nothing spending water
over fisted creek
my lover's voice, her visage

out of time singularly implored
comforts a poverty
clayed

slips heavy
from its casing. The population
of the world
commences

YELLOW FIELD

One pole strung
with wire on the crest
of a hill. In this light

all I can see.

nothing grows, the legend

cut changes minds, not minds
abbreviated to sell tedium.
Afternoon the Morning contradicts, yet behind it some in-
tention
laws

to piss, to question behavior, to
rise at five to walk to work, carefully parsing verbs
the tribal history in photographs

a hill that rose, rises, perhaps
the remembered color walled
on wall off even
when it rises clear before no one,

the guards
are delicious
inaudible
lyric

for the rest are stories everyone
but me
knows
from the steps where fallen scrip for a rewrite
buys these days? Whatever the have-nots

mumbo-jumbo terror outside town declined
a job in no position, or produced
a story counter to the brotherhood. Justice won't condone a metaphor. Breaks we
give what words to change choose rattles in gunny, weights attached. Restraint,
child. Your script's about done. Suit private ideology slapped opinion polls with
tickets to the informants, trading ID's an Army helicopter at the treetops, feel our
thunder. Wake
up in a cot
sweating
at the typewriter

angels
ring
the letter "P",
the manacles, the grating

lies, I suspect, when spoken
to.

PRIVATE LIFE

To dis-
bridge men to me detach column lines we hook-up daily. To discrete roles at the elaborate cornice, of the antic carved there, on my trade sworn. As a thief sworn among crud where I
would hide my one
true habit
more to shame than its interior
appointments, one
by one and each
more solid
lasts tended out of water. I may lose consciousness, but society continues. Fare time to linger over souvenirs. A kind of property gone to tenements match esteem to clutter. I'll trade sepia vote for higher octane. In this society the old men lead
lean into fire
as the meat
allows. The choice begins come home in a box. Take a number at the door. A job's a job but on your profile over hobby find ability to kill. I'll be tanked by dawn and down to the plant
erased
my neck, what's good
for the country
stamped
grade by lottery
assumed, according to shoot straight mythological hardons six for a buck. Not enough to sell my sex option out of pocket. I may not own the language but the meanings are mine. Whose homogeneity? Fear of the tube to jump cut some
emotional
dysfunction
am dying

where I live powerless
to stop my hands
shaking, breath shallow
this calling on its orbit falters. Sow contentment to your sleeve when to the crowded marketplace you balk at history. What reference? What past doing something completely original. Start naming the birds. I'm in this body, door locked, economy, of the illusion.

up short on him
question-like
to avoid traps
advantage the arctic
man or wolf does what he wants
a surfaces
incrementally
all of them a unit moving
there, there
using English on the prow
to generalize
his kind
allegiance be fed
through the teeth
caution
out this stranger's back door
brick yard
foot's a loose
hands wrenching up lugs
cheaply
pried and scattered
members called other stops
on entering
uneasy
talk in the depressions gathered
out of rope
itched
up creek to throw
a sentence
quickly cored
to cacophony's
mazes
trusts accuser's
lip, sect
and depend
indentured

FIGURES

Fix your eyes.
Careful

a characteristic gesture, a tic has soiled utility. Pare off what's intended to the true routine. In this scene shank rests left right left right an idiosyncratic sway to the pelvis like grinding his teeth. What sounds destined's but the next corner, arriving tired.

Figures of production. The terms mean less when used. Listen to the facts pulling a needle through my cloth. Too often short of breath. Fact compacting needle's skill puts to run, a daily threat. Rules to live by

observing any given
through

But I'll embellish what I see, seeing in fact sentiment.

resistance, not as stone, but stone
better left

At the instant of discrimination, at the seed of the rationale, fist over hand. Who holds out his hand? Who's paying? Payment is artifice. Their linkage is linguistic, poverty as well of the same equation. Agreement of violence

Knowing what a knife cut
too keep the place clean

Don't rest. Don't describe. You won't fail but be burned.

to empty
my life

cautious to the last atom
nesia's implied to stay alive

Debunking spiritual poverty as a thing not yet successfully defined, sup with us. Do you know where your next meal is coming from? We're like any company, but better. Who'll say grace?

My can't help comparing mine with theirs. I continue shrinking. I am taller, taller by far. Do you like the way I strut and spit?

POOR

got
his
angry

touched pissed his leg deprived. Common to the victim completes the characterization. Summed for the instrument, run down revving or after work, the mechanics of bubble-packing burned in. One day the man'd

to represent a class. But the boss can't be bought. In our
memory

saved a wheel's purpose
between
my hands
a metal
cut

man hours
of making of the oozy glass
vials in obscurity
for the Greater

nods, or nearly does, as from on high, acknowledging his vague imprisonment. He paces in his chair. All of one Good, the machine's a fetter to his arm, an example from a great house to these little tics. He looks directly at me. The condition

dismisses its containment. Orders from semen, from bile and vinegar. From no liquid wrapped in pincers to adopt and overthrow its purpose. Divide and subdivide, and at the end of sleeping,

curls a knuckle down
white street
working off a
cattle prod a gang inline
devotion

of the attitudes his prayers
are catalogued,
discarded.

YELLOW FIELD

bitter pronoun
lost
a pellet

standing by a given
name
like acid

from the brow
down
an insufficient

figure ground
such pleasure the teeth
permit

from coalescing
shit to eternity
oppose

iconophratry to determination
dies,
another forms, like

excrement
no part
kin to me

here aching
hole
in evil as in water

tamed irony
counts
pulses

off among flies
wonderfully organized
after suicide

combining
in a digit
all that in a pit

confounds
entry
to interior

ferns and mucus
swell to dull
sense

PROFESSIONAL

extent the fingers
with instruments tests
precise coordination to the job

saving lives, minds
charmed or lost brotherhood
in comparable

soul careers. Ghost
the little attitudes up
from the envelope

times boredom equals
by birth conflicted
prized truce. It didn't

work then nor will
to talk of other than compromise
it later than you think

STINGERE

Heat
seeking the remittance
ocorpse on's levied
heavily
door to door-wise clogs
th'exhaust dammy
switched-on middle class
ablowin arap conned particulate
disreputes iheap
up's profits n'exports pollutes
'em outta fruits
labor tunneling they heirs'
chances used
up atom amode ander
snatch inna oven tooths
jagged be commerce inter
alia buys
another year avoids
s'subject enactor inner
ther sunset fullogrit
fer guy/girl counter pores
outta livin po nasty squeams
the rigger t'be A number one
k'next n'next n'next stampun um
offer xerox gunning exxons
ybloat. Unguent
to legion apply blame
affixed patch at bachy
gearjawin abt bein teed
awhile shunne plants

waging bi-cuts er
wortless shim beem attitude
t'counter pain offolk
ammedic an actuary recollect
per court o'co. 's'side ever
enna bleed
smeared occult off
cited nat'l sec'ty oft
eds til calmed
and spread buboes arrest.
A pin prick enneed manifold
strung to caps
fumes ababes bonfire
outpacing thism's supporate
promises aware sin fluence tobacco
whiskey poor iconography
emmesms whip hour
will to a wire
heat teach uns burnin a taut
scar rapid suck
umbrage wade out sustained
on market day
be crimmen skirmish enaddled
sold ardour
to bussy a fect'l
collapse astride empires
alies greeds many small
pustular ends.

SHUTTLE CHALLENGER

red glare
image enhanced

in awe the nation's payload
plume at 59.262 divergent
yaw and pitch

in air gave proof
bombs
cheer

the military workhorse
throttled up
to milliseconds

lost
for their country in God
Wars

consolidated wealth tooled
up in space struts

Control to see the right solid rocket booster
gleaming

"How many centipedes went under the wall when he came in? Better to pick her up by the ears. When thunder comes in over the hills I feel big, then I feel small. Thirty steps from here to the house. A few more will be alright."

Here, the sunlight like a bed sheet. Arrogance act to know a man, perhaps confide in him, and then to come upon him by surprise, talking to strangers in another language. He is an enemy. Kill him and there will be another, perhaps many more.

"Not my logic. I'm a crocodile. Recognize me? Gnawing on a green twig. A perfect liar."

Watched *Miami Vice*. Had a drink. Took a shower. Got to chill out. It's all in the way you carry yourself. They're hung up in debate. Let's get

Threat of the Good Example. With an average attention span of 11 seconds. Snub out that cigarette; not bad for a gink. I'll make a clock in that foliage. Cut it! Hard it is just to talk. Whose hair is this? It's matted, bloody.

Not a person on the streets, all boarded up, not even a dog. There are no maps and no telephone service. Aim for their accomplishments, their school or granary. No more general talk. Back home they've got all the answers and they're all wrong. This detail feels good, my legs under me as I stand up and start walking.

"The story is she'd been to Nicaragua, and had gotten sick. She'll dance like that for a couple of hours. That was a year ago. Sweating. She laughed, really a full laugh, and then she dropped."

Each comes with his own presumptions. That's a hindrance gunfire drops. Call a doctor. The more you understand, the less you want to come here. And no support from home.

STATUS

About, within me sounds, metal seizing and releasing
devils knocks a racist percept
off a ledge, the barrio alive over heaving by.
Mine with fluorocarbons, byproduct of a dance
that fascinates me. In its lives of the third
person gratified and hid needy. More needy
came to rob me, picked my
pocket wage I'd traded a wife, little pick
the kid's drug hunger. And I am similar;
the population produced that aberration
in the gut strung for sale.

Midway on the path of cast
lots remembering my name that no guide's
dropped his kindly prod to trust me
loose on any African street, to watch
imagining orders fail to coalesce. Stone
color of lard begs a vandal. Why should I
cut wrists to name an heir as firing layabouts
hacked a city in its sleep. Days each waited
with the rest, wearing nothing, full of blood rubbing
back his chafes. Nights rifle our camps, no harm.

I won't apologize. None to advantage but the spot
price of oil, and exhausted at that
copped this attitude. There's birds in the highway
stick up your wallet, the Bastard, I can see him
almost clear! Then he gets away.

Don't notice we've trench in the Township puddle
of warm and muddy drink with pride
out of my all summer. Divided against
the went down, the way their children
group at the pool, not remarkable, really,
when my neighbor steals and tells.
An armed vehicle leads the water tank.
No, I know it wasn't always so, but so
five died since Tuesday. The president
delirium on its pivot sits like an image
over fuming. Past the heat
distortion three men load a metal chest.

Stink endured a character of its own, increasing its demands
past five. Allowed to club greed.
More propaganda footage turned
with the public ugly, or rather, refined to the same
end, habit, blunt, leader of exiles.
How's the cult? Hold the pill
under your tongue kills fleas like me, Bigshot.
Remember, I earned my money
cables Yalta with a change of plans
advanced wipe out a village. Breaths in a
hole underground, a tin bunker.

Some recommendation, to say I've got feelings
a line of tenements a brickyard
kicks like yesterday's mule. Interior
ex-child takes any blame, a cockroach
from the food chain fixed watching.

Denounce my fragments among and scolding the "conveniences
to pollute, a mechanical lens off stage. Put my face there
the plate drops, molded lead.
Damn the fuckers make a profit off it up
prop mustard rain in a ghetto, stay in today.

My wit and my ability compressed to a shovel's
blade against the supple wounded, never
under capitalism boasted these directives
folded, brushed, and laid upon the fire.
Hunger calling talent to fish it up
to an erection. Get it? You
already got off in New York, but hey,
it's a job you say your storehouse
to storehouse of elevated purchase, shooting it out.

Can I trade force, pass it on to an empty
chamber tenant? Inside her stiff at a long
indifferent stretch, becoming money
quick to sterile with the Lord's work.
Silver latent in me, lost
combination of humors rules
the world broke killing me.

I'm not done carving my leg. Not done
proper name's fetus yields
8% drawn and quarter compound
the insult won't give birth. Leave one ink
for another, sicken from that one, leave
it running into the earth at my feet.
I've got nothing more to say. Dig elsewhere.

that is uncompleted, day
to another age my life in a mirror
obeys, as if there were laws to the succession

events not counted in greatness, which greatness,
articulated, is its own vulnerability.

From proliferate
meaning what is behind every treet, some danger
revealed. The pleasure

bring in the first person I see,
at another tale, separated from me
by a device. Practice

myself the little wand
arc where ought be sky, burn
awkwardly in love, in trying

Wheel

for Julia

Chax Press

1992

(Prints by Gil Ott, from the letterpress book printed in Tucson, Arizona, at Chax Press, by Charles Alexander. Originally *Wheel* included seven additional pages. Later these pages became a part of the book *Traffic*, and appear here on pages 205-208.)

can talk with a living, but not with a dead

man would to

me, you, and the rest, the present

face, the population changes

knowing it

easy, after
ambiguity's been cheated.
The fat calf's slaughtered

first to deplete

the difference between those born on one continent

moving from anger among us

with dignity the sentence

coupled in ways
to retain clarity characteristic
of a seed, a memory

shed, crumbles ahead. What's
set to killing cannot of itself
the rites

proclaim skimmed off or on tension,
accumulate name and brake
primitive

rules apply. Simple simple. I came to question

history exclude the vanquished, each false

mountain or tree, or species

manufactured item, until so much
of nature and of human endeavor

return its gaze. They have imitated
our dress, and our manneer

in public sought signs in other's

wind determine
how to speak
knocked out of me

furrows, which, after rain, lost

lay down in

The Whole Note

Zasterle Press

1996

1 / 4

Our sea, to rough trade cautiously approached. Pea green and troughing, sounds like poetry. There's a license finds me

at wild anise, out this window facing one of all the hills to the sea run. Prominent stalk to yellow promise, ordered and notified. Able solitary laws to grow in me

excrescent, damned, never enough. Exterior to year's own narrative, one's evolving miscalculated hunger, or hunger's tumor. Weed be beautiful, be beauty, dependent

simply in anticipation of youth drummed everywhere but home. Take and use. Discriminate. As in laying,

scrape up art from surfaces unbidden. My body standing next, compared to what a wild seed produced. I walk away.

Fastened by bones to the hillside, feeding cypress. Apt secrets revealed by looking, instead of looking at, fill my silhouette.

Control's conceit, out of each substance's specificity gobbled, flickers at the idea. I feel a rod in me, that would stand against a claw, afield. The sanitary arguments of home

pure mathematics fill a bag. More nettle than tooth, anxiety than the strength summoned during yesterday's possession dries in its relation. Poverty, from my wife and family separated

for batting, forgiving the very thorns that wreck my sleep. Longer surviving

figuring it out, troubling the wound to outlast me. Spar for it. Can codify uncertainty here in the nearer acreage, albeit inaccurately, these deities.

The first child chosen us to fret, from its advance with eucalyptus to the grove's edge, leaping out of the condensery! Tracking honorable meat, deserts nested.

on coupled abilities. Welcome to this image of yourself, sure as I imagine you. Your little peals

part, whole scrabble to douser under scrubby sage. Free me,

I say with your intention equals gender. Until you light, investing the common, redeemable dream.

My love, in all my imperfection, are here, despite your attribution to another entry. Less than breeze, than presence, the transmission

circles like a hawk, or any other problem set to right

candles to tense, in our knowledge of each other, three. This difficulty multiples a pinpoint phrases, care taken in song's revolve. My rider has descended, you

recede and grow numerous. Night, the sky with milk by dropper, not to locate you, but waste. Of all representatives

the last to leave, chances, dedicated.

Not to think of

for which there were need. Unguided and without attitude toward the brush land,
or other men, sing incapable of singing. It is your way interacting out of

safety, the parallel strides that in the end lead… where? The sense of what is not
of for the next meal the exact pose establishes. Going to

landscape, to be approached benignly, which specificity sat on the brow, devil,
cool air from then cave

indifferent admonishes no one. Cry for a stiff throat, glide to another branch.
Find me wandering plans to interrupt decay.

The length of my stride cored for pulp, for the preservation of abstractions. Owl
to range, I've sacrificed

lone affirming, mauled and bleed, for some orderly apocalypse. The grove darken
covers a loom that operates here. The leaf, but its possessor do not dance

outside of this familiar to me. Try my arms, the height of my hips' measure to sap

sentences lacking subject, predicate, equilibrium, a pace implies home, identity,
mine determined

to undermine a diagram. Heel to ball. Forward heedless of the intrusion on
purview, compromised.

Stop and way eager to follow a yellow bird. A little dry

seeded where the seed fell absolute. The nothing intimate alone in break day
clapped the door behind me, shot out on own free will. Fox is not always easily

my name, to irritate my man. Power over wants to stroll all puffed up, a caricature.
My disagreeable bifurcation as well. Tiring to cleave

aback moss, shade and distance. Were to work it off hung of the crowd, timed
by seasons of rain. Your injury opportune only as support can wax. Otherwise,
I'm still looking for parables

light away. The house and settlement are empty, destined their inhabitants. Sharpen
my plan, an image of hunting.

First to write them, then get to know the less and less form assuming. Poem to
another auditor: prayer, chant, lecture lovingly assembled. When will you tell me

the time it took to find that skull, to carry it home. Altar became dumb need for
a fly whisk. More private, all you've written, founded on

volume than blood. Pine needle loft, a few yards away, liveforever

my last sight. Scratchings became my left foot scared awake. Hopping in panic
a physical rag dripping rum

paper to air ignite, abrade my body. Shadow passing sun passing shadow. I'm here
somewhere you're talking to

pace in a circle, scheme, while there is still light.

2 / 4

Each sustained gaze deflected, feminine for shame. Contemplative or active
operation on a wave from multiple to indicated tread water resists through
indirection. Unbalanced to the next

without a subject, belonging elsewhere. What profit from a poem, or picking
starfish from the hair

of one collapsed at last stagger. Water is one fills the concave on the corpse removal,
is many

sensate at play, fools surviving in a column of words. Clarifying anger adoring gold,
at a little fish beached a principle affirmed and broken. Break off sleep to sleep
purposeful wander.

Bark and fennel stalk destroyed, scattered scent winding in the same field the
violent

macadam, wires and traps. Monotone and irrational acts listen this bag of ribs
is letting wind! By hurry

mean debacle at hand. Transform in habits a colony, tests his vocal cords, cries
out at the people who invented him. In every case the imperative case

too to wait for rain and be a part of nothing. Muscle in the skin pull to a gait
presence, even

surface and interior. Night is more familiar, run ordered there. Lacking breath,
redirect wit.

His own neighbor to appear himself uplifted, and elsewhere, victim of the theft erodes way of going under. I meet him on an isolated corner, we exchange

punctuation to intelligible adjustment, through his eyes. Compare paranoia, twice

old bird out of hell to ruminate alone. Up and express my will his habits contemn my knowledge of his failing

exposed. In his ease those listening as well, a board stick jammed where bone had been, the crown of a tooth

spat blood, or rum, collapsing, then standing again. The steps, once lost, are never exhausted. The youthful look a drug deserts wants in, that is, out with me, from here.

Full of paper's bobcat spot verified by previous sightings. The cat's intelligenced a man of the state where none was sustained. Danged friable paths and utter

fixed attends a slight sway, a quick glance left and staple on. Bulk obscured by chaparral, that dried by drought, a shuffle the weight

tread and threat preparing. Ennerved pace like the earth a minute

two, there, by the scent, flanks exposed. The text is nothing, not even waiting. Taste lost sleep

a tense identity violating mere whereabouts, careful to back off still. An apt slip, game, and the brush runs by.

Not that it can't be, but I can't tell you. Disturbance to my foot print scrapes narrative assumptions, breath knuckled by labor. Analyze <<disturbance>> and find its regularity

proven in the inhabitant need. Solidity the aura reminds an absence a place to hide. The molted

annual crop leaps. Fog from skirts tiny warm differential peeps, a kind of secret, vestige

surviving out of the picture. Nourishment and patience fall shadow to your eagerness to know. Length a day out under camouflage, attributed odors daily twists out of reach. Sink a lair, decay.

I make a sound. I am out of breath, always, my sound becoming a complaint, my complaint

hump, moving through the fog. Fear asleep swim obsessed with enforcing rhythm. Wounded and taken, held

to own a scar, pilloried to be fed is no possession. I to those I associate adventure and routine, uncertain in memory. From them one, all of us available

at distances uncommonly dissolved. Black in my eye, gone, an angular trespass frozen against me. Night's water's cape, have at me, all you want, exhaust and further.

Another man, a woman, with effort, confess effort physically construed. The breathing

column parallel truths lain by the expiring do, what must be done. Walking in silence, at ability joyous, to muscled speech. Operative we, the varieties of pace argue and agree

height, endurance, knowledge of causes sure to divide we bring and bring it up without departing. What difficulty

spurious flight, glide beckoned, the crevice, creek and marsh coincide. Certain light disturbance or character of wind to human presence, full of face constituted, abbreviated choice. We to they web carrion, walking still.

May be right, were I closer. Signifying not at all or everything evades identification at wing a quarter mile away. I take time writer to sit, remove you to whom

magnified parceling you out teases alterity. World one in a grid spies the natural it out of it filth. Reading feces artifact customs are traded to dominate, again, to suggest a safe distance. Causes presupposed a chance to return

end, and simultaneously finite the subject of classification can't rebel. Accepted becoming

of those to whom I don't speak, to join these desired. My daily appetite insults a system. Grace at prey, convective after.

3 / 4

Of use to dead souls, cloth leached and summoned, errant. Steps prescribed, resistance turns a minor note the gathered

in animal defense and leaf-mask imagine their own terror. The stale scent, foul breath, enliven the rags' challenge

ritual shame marked in time to ring in. Full aware, corrupting a meal the poor to regulate and to exhaust. A vision is dark, liquid

agitate the length a night throes horribly until dawn contained. Reduced to a twitch in bed

gray authority fail to confer, withdraw. One familiar function after taken over, abrupted, suffer one forgotten verse.

Habiting the stall, inkling who, to whom I'll receive my utilization. Will to erase will be damaged by orthodoxy. Sitting still and complicated

beginning, out of us shocked a full life. Pulled, to say all the go deny, spin convulse and fall saying <<These excesses

are mine. Your rendering

withholding rightfully my livelihood to waste, strut and goad. In me the many sources of laughter coalesce. Chuck by gambol

atop poverty indifferent to rape the conduct I came out of. Striving to kick returns with each encounter hovers edge of us, a crowd or stand care less about them, you, friend.

In shouts, in actions, vague potentialities pass into circular imitation. Always here and now, the inventing

looking for itself, and back again fearing and drawn. Half a day spun fenced to burn individual meat, acting out me, the author, the pleasure of every company. Who are hidden

themselves rooms delineate none of the mass. At 'em each by hundreds spit spirited crows. Cede nothing, I'm separate from

penetrate my limbs, cross against my will. Fault synesthesia, within at heights dumb from looking down

shaken to relief. Apply mud paste, repeating its name, tense haunched off in the yard alone.

W/thanks to Dr. Louis Mars, *The Crisis of Possession in Voodoo*, Reed, Cannon and Johnson Publishing, 1977.

This feeble stick, this debris. Pry with a twig the mass a ready man dances to reconcile sounds from a rural grave with vacant unison. He is revealed

spirits demanded split from the grove of hands to burn, incarnate, white up a sweat. Name deity the rounds of the blank assembled to charge fealty with alcohol, poverty to congregate

penury undone. Out of the blood a knife's work freed him for these rounds, and unmarked he every mark inspected. Glazed

the city of souls thick dependence momentarily undone. Raw sensory equivalence an animal tongue, a limp or worse affliction raises the dead among us. Harm and again relieved.

Did not attain, attain or vacate, is has no momentary need to be digested. At this corner the valley in shadow, day sweeps up, exposed. Were ten days passed

brief dust accumulated a test of sense only, were failed. Noticed but did not record

futility in describing the mount, some particle of dirt talking in tongues. Mockery street's small faces crowded up offering themselves

ample weather change emptied the vehicle that it could be roughly seized, and stayed, sustaining the posture over time. No whisper. Explaining cartilaginous fuses adequacy, the sitter, thin milled timber smashed contending.

From oneself counting, a way to figure rain, up night cause of the estrangement. The word sours, jealous

of the fever to exacerbate one's head. Walking around delinquent, susceptible. Catch him off guard to move in

pairs bare character that is a god and clay gone rank. One equals a sum of transgressions tricked in the crotch

in public. Eating the meat meant for poorer imposters drags his wooden foot

rub the formal aspects of the dance, the couples and small groups going on lightly. Fabric rip by singing a dare to the accuser, as if no one notices.

Remote home coaxed out of the dark, glossolale to fix it. The rider has a job to do, and uses all stoking reck and, should the horse be

able. How were you planned? Same here sealed in longing, accessible only

spurs to indolence up heat chastisement. Getting there get angry bleat out the human box mangles its prey. Residence bone and nerve scuff on purer air. Slide

truncate spirit, invent a future compass, a milk. So it is amnesia

sentences out of youth. The hole this morning fills with trembling made the passage, marked by all but absent son. Call the scar your son.

Emptied with a tug floats over intention. Numb to opportunity, feeling the constraints form

imposes, wayfaring. The last hour, caught not looking for an answer's a kestrel, nesting in the cornice. Aren't they beautiful answers which flee their trace How faster

from which a poem, out of identical anguish. Lightweight, out of control, moved

to panic, waking late. A convincing wisdom, walk into the fire. What other choice peeled off behind me, me again.

4 / 4

Moving, variant ornithography of those uninitiated

made into memory by the me briefly incarnate. Full of myself on successive nights dense and alone sings

you back. Need keeps the book of dying open, the language common after all. Relieved, the task finally changing prompts tapping my reserve

feeling, now, wise to its edge. Where are you risk any detail of what's in me, having been tricked by the image of a man. Softly pain the intuit

applications under authority of breathing. I drive this one, I get winded

calendar's familiar, speed and abruption.

Of one's existence, adopted to debility to have it out of silage steeping, inescapable. Onto one woman

another inequity hoped to thirty to settle. Cripple, for the platen his chest opened, the emote standing in phials reminiscent

indomitable due free movement among bodies, that waits and will absorb that's dished. Christian to these passions

without time this time the visitor will burn along forced choice of hosts. Virtue to heat, crumble, pass as the village forgets

he still walks unassisted. Minded the story of a life he'd got foot on, so careful.

In the round of abnegate scoring among locking peer workers, demands and their deceptions, love made

torn, at times, out of wallcovering, animated to destroy my own house. As from a wallet, applied simile fond, a sense of mission. Sincerer kin cop to my survival in secrets. Hell sounds

capable over a pit losing everything. Gentle evolved

self of absolutes absolute congruence this then repeated discovery. Wake to me aisle between waking us simultaneously. A slot for putting worry came to pray

with effort out of a role. Foretold the under this chair I sit on, humbled and green, and gray.

Descend, or overturn a temporary order for a cold one. An opening is in or out testing the condition run

my skin off, free of constraint. Blind me at speeds my legs toward enduring. Of my antithesis

scrawl wasting who said patiently absorbing? Scrabble in any direction glory little, like a squirrel. Path of indifference, subtending achievement equally

opaque. Without me, you

trunk, stone, cave entire to chance and chance cohesion of mind. The warrant at dark, and that early.

And the little wind ran, animating random. Sluggish, count warmth in a scrap I'm breathing the regular foam

gutter, iron to crease anger. Weight to conform all workers' surprise at the appearance of the sun. Another day. Pad flat

the curse the bit of sidewalk soaks craving liquid. Heavy, bulk, a state all interior coat over

head and feet skewed toward no meal. Dancing this way to beg me, muscle is common. Some air, that too

private decay, the eloquence of concern. Piled on every bone felt, and beside me, unexpected, me.

In whose ears the ringing ebb hid, a shadow moving on the sidewalk. Quick amid a piecemeal sea that's come to inhabit

gently by the throat. Age by age, a syllogism to the sounding bow grows deeper as the stop moves on, the interior

with difficulty to any appointment crumbles. What protected artery this weak, human circumstance advances the distance resonance marks. Today, this one end

the knees fed paste and chore. Back at centuries, bone inserted

bruise and get away, the interior recovered. Drink lesser, rested vapor.

Part by part removed, the pleasures first. How at the end the inhabitant looks on past habitation

treed, out of breath, less permanent affecting landscape than its cold lake or hill. Dark walk on

leak blood. Dispassionate grace the water's edge

reach to what hypothesis uncertainty led the spirit. Still, moving, speaking, incomprehensible. Feet set in mud, decayed, and other feet

tirelessly composed. From lap and slaver crusts tenuously amid succeeding motilities endure, some history, any. Fear, but fear's

subject unremembered, everywhere present.

Prone to the observance, a formal end only, blurred with or without morphine decides to live. I have made a mistake, a meandering

stasis, down a notch and starting over. Someone else's surgery pulled a knot out, left a man handled roughly

bumped and thrown what dirt brackets. Possessed of this violence, a plea remains. Fed on seed here, a small black bird

far and still admissible. I will build a body of utterance, that fooled me. The odor will stay, and I

will walk away.

Traffic

Chax Press

2001

. . . each individual has his own personal measure of time that depends on where he is and how he is moving.

Stephen Hawking, *A Brief History of Time*

FREQUENCIES

Fourteen years ago I arrived at the form of the *Traffic* poems. It was intended to allow me to explore two modes of writing: purely observational, line-based verse, and more reflective, sentence-based "poet's prose." Constituted of short poems and fragments, the form offered a further solution to me as I moved through my thirties, with the accretion of relationship and responsibility concomitant to that age, and with increasingly diminished "free" time for writing. It permitted me to take advantage of random moments in a busy life: commutes to work, waiting for the rice to boil, a cup of coffee in a busy shop, etc. The time frame for production has been of no concern. I was to write 80 poems (an arbitrary number, no doubt influenced by Zukofsky's then-recent *80 Flowers*), adhering to no unifying theme of narrative development.

By the natural force of the mind making whole, however, the collection (it is not a "series") has found its unity, not so much in its form as in the chunk of time that it has come to occupy. It is for me a personal time, a bracketed identity, beginning mid-stride in my formative years as a poet, and ending no less abruptly with Charles Alexander's offer to produce the book, and my subsequent refining and polishing of the final manuscript. For the reader who would read the entire collection, or any discrete piece of it, the effect will be similar.

This is not an inflated claim. I have always felt that the challenge in reading poetry is equal to or greater than that of writing it. The "poet" is not so much the one who composes or delivers the work, nor the one who reads and interprets, but the mutual establishment of all of these.

This, then, is Traffic's life in time. The short, repeated form permits a briefest asusmption of subject, with a puzzling suggestion of reiteration or commentary in the prose. The cumulative effect is strobe-like. But as a whole, and without my authorization, the poems combine to fill up space, and to suggest a larger stride.

Time is, of course, experienced in a multitude of ways, from the ephemeral to the immovable. The time taken up by a dream, for instance, may be expanded indefinitely and never exhausted. The time of grief, on the other hand, or of love, has a solidity and opacity that test endurance.

This latter, more solid experience of time is the realm of fate, or memory, of obsession and aspiration, and other descriptive constructs of the mind. It is no less ephemeral, for being solid, than is the moment just past, which cannot be grasped. But it does seek distinction in the mind, which is to say that it spreads and covers all of existence, which we then explain in terms of duration and depth.

It would seem to be a universal human desire to believe, in the face of all contravening evidence and the complexity of the present moment, in a stable world, near at hand, or attainable only through long struggle, a sentimental or instructive past or a future utopia. That past and future are essentially fictions is the fact that their theoretical presentation as symmetry and dichotomy is intended to obscure. The concept of a present as a divider, or a mirror with past and future reaching out from a neutral vanishing point, denies the authority of the mind, which is only alive now.

These conflicting impulses are, in essence, our grappling with time, a condition which we experience only on a subjective, multivalent level. In the interest of sustaining a belief in something larger than this experience, we attribute duration and frequency to the moment. Taken to an extreme, these frequencies divide into pure verb and non-referential qualifier: living – alive; moving – static; sensing – ecstatic; etc. Despite its promise, the gerund expires as the pairing of which it is a part separates and dissolves. Language, the act, is present, while articulation, the echo, cannot be.

The skin fell
from her young face.
None of the others
noticed. Talking of children.

Where sky and the earth meet, where all materials are finally exhausted; these which had been perceived as limits provide companionship. White, walking the face of a mountain in the clouds. Deep love for the thought of a twig in the sand.

Two men's faces
in the night
in the doorway
red.

If it has happened, it is complete. Where a rock stood, there is no longer a rock. Speaking about it, the subject changes.

The sound of a scissor
in her voice. An advancing
spot of light she spoke of
hoped to betray.

Where there is no reference for love, all that surfaced in suspect advances. Tone and depth, all qualities of the woman like the play of shadows in a pond. provoke a madness of conclusion. A word; nowhere to rest.

Trying to sleep, but aware
of the room.

based on the most commonplace
traffic, unwilling.

When the sleeping one wakes, all the paranoia of Europe were his. The chair, tree and landscape resist; only patterns seem brilliant, and fade.

He cries or laughs in the room above.

War is the
topic of sages
rare
uses for bayonets.

All the faculties of the healthy man are also in the service of the solider, and are especially acute due to the deprivation of his spirit. Poets have praised these virtues.

Proportionately, calf to thigh, bent,
to chest to arms, hands joined lightly on the chest,
pleasing, alone.
Without strength, breathing on the blue
uneven concrete.

Unashamed, we eat the same meal. All the art of the moment is open to use.

At the window
birds

Easily a 100 of us inside
could hear them.

Brothers and sisters came into the room and established their stations. From the center we stepped it out, they stepped it out. Aurora. The poles of our work, until we chose to end, were maintenance and invention.

before the child is born.

Her tongue
in the cavity of her mouth,
tropical rain.

The useless, the outer part, which had given color, discarded. had the unborn distinguished between the apparent and the not-seen, how it would have laughed! Then the fruit itself is taken into the mind.

When the cold had
fully penetrated he began to shiver

lake
he'd circled on foot.

What does it mean, "to shiver?" Shivering, the yard seemed tamed, the lake a circle.

Comparison
and independent

One "to" and "to," the other "among," I said
"are not equal," neither did
they

White and black, and at the edges, sepia. These men, in the excellence of their language, have not yet touched. The snow that falls when they are still, the sensation. Black.

close before he woke
got up and left. In the middle of the day
one lie

It will not be reconciled before he sleeps. If there is only one pleasure, he will find others.

toward the tree in the dark lot where her clothes
had been thrown

step after step

eyes raised to the horizon.

The eyes take more than their share. At the threshold your guests suddenly harden, yet continue to move forward. Attend them now.

about her, to the cup
that still held a bit of her coffee.
or care of men, opinion
that moved me

to no common life, I listened

This spot or that, as if a "spot of light" were something of substance! In the negative dream her face is horrible, and turns away.

String, meat, she laughed, the yellow
wall behind her in her
glass of water.

So empty, that glass, it presents no challenge to her specificity. So many of her, glass surfaces, she takes a complement to the words of her admirer. He is divided, and becomes himself.

the lights at two
in the afternoon. last

fire had burned a worm shape
in the leaves when no one

here today.

proven otherwise. What occurs is of it. Here, some blood was absorbed, and the place has grown bigger to accommodate it; there, an encounter.

morning
beacon

reaches forward, and back
to a time separated, a dominating

saddened by the light which washes its
approach, suppress the gain

She climbed on top of me without saying a word, without breathing. There was nothing playful about it. I thought to open my eyes, but she moved skillfully between them and the source of light from the window. I stayed in the dream.

Susan ran to the empty hallway
following a scream

was alive.
identical brown wood doors, and a light

There is no puzzle here; it is all self-evident. The witness also bears guilt. She tells and retells, looking for that same light.

least of all the seasons

to the recapitulated

time of life he turned a corner
on a street in a city
he had seen

spoken of her father's seizure, which he'd witnessed more than fifteen years before. "When pain doesn't make any promise to leave. It takes all of your concentration; you have to be casual."

what of greater interval
to attack, a punk I didn't see
than the exposure, winter

Time is the apparent vacuum, the passage of seasons. Gratitude for the violent in love and property. In the architecture of the gap, they are doors.

finger pressed to the neck
base of the skull.
                                        a moon
cold and clear

initiated. Panic as the occasion for refusal grows increasingly remote. The sound of the door closing corresponds with an awareness of dark shapes at the edge of the field. Another passage, thinking.

planes of her shin, her upper
arm where it meets her shoulder and disappears
behind the glare of the automobile

window. Determined
by the camera, her fingertip and field
she deletes.

The economy of the sexes stirs in that neutrality, that were not spoken stand against four qualities of light. I have written

The three drops left
in your mouth, the three

chairs, mornings, letters
nothing for it if it isn't
approximate

The same man disagreed who abhorred sentimentality. In a dance the two were reconciled, but their satisfaction faded in the way one understands a death, or wishes to, and then falls out of understanding.

dye either
washed out or bleached
by the sun
to be told "no."

A shattered bone. The risks I'd taken multiplied, bothered to answer them. They pass, from chlorine to the mountains, and then to the sky. That's all I know.

I can't say

the doctor to his patient, an exchange
of cards

limited to one, to wife, to no other

the pride I felt when events changed, and my opinion prevailed. After the fact, he caught on and, to a more permanent wisdom. He cut back. The rowing made us both tired. We looked for opportunities to rest.

locked the door early

waited in the car until she

looked, directly

tired, music a habit
impeded by circuit design

projected rate of return

required a personality

He put on his clothes very deliberately, so that I questioned our intimacy. Yet the beauty of his movements, in which he believed, taking him further

effort of listening, the undivided

manifest in a speech you are not fit
to teach or practice. And yet

now, in the inflection of your lip,
the mutability

To say disappointment is not a thing I can see and touch? Sometimes your intelligence is not equal to what you know.

permit her to listen
to her mother's

I think in the metal of it, the trigger and bore. Like laughter from the next table. The girl is fascinated, and wants to have a conversation with the rift.

He would not walk with me beyond the fallen
tree that marked his neighbor's

not yet out of winter.
What I'd gone out to think about

me to go after what I want. Harmed, of other purposes. The line would sometimes pull taut, and stay that way, and only gradually fall slack. I really don't have a chance."

We had to drive through a slum
to get

without cause. She simply
paused in her story, then picked it up

In retrospect, I can see how I have negotiated with my own poverty. I've apologized, and have accepted a sense of self-guidance. The work is not yet over. We make a world, each of us, from unrelated fragments.

perceived my intention, and
spoke of it.

Pale figure, breathing
toward sleep

three form a coda, to take out of code, over all memory you've brought to these poems. "…who mastered it so well in their previous lives that they only need… a word or two…." Distinguished by their grace, three, on a cusp, without predicate

far away, he is, although
he is sitting at my feet

my privacy. His question is familiar, rephrased, and he takes pride simply in having asked it. I haven't yet formed my question. Under what other circumstances could I not have loved

rested, but still furiously
out of breath. Black bud of leaves wave
within range

taken sparingly, gain in significance. Choice of poverty affirms abundance. My perspective is certain; it is the same seed in me. It wants to go outside to love me, and so comes between

cries, reaching
into the stroller.
What must have been a book, the way it crumbled

privately her

by on the street. I can't hear myself, can't be heard. Dismayed and relieved another pronoun turning paper.

As will be demonstrated

seeing the spider stops

reaching for his name:
father, authority, peer

beneath the virtual scar
hard blood

It does no good to choose one impression to represent a multitude of events. A exemplify infinity, yet in congress arbitrate paradigm. In the book encode it: "My eyes meet those of another man in a public place. We do not look away."

She's here. Hold

in my hand, that comprehensible

image, weight and intent her

true record left fixed

light and shadow, the muscle

bought relaxes. We'd make

Succession of faces over eight pages. If you can pay for it,you have every right. You're a fool if you can't decide. Watch your finger-prints. The paper alone is enough."

sheet to the line, perspective

in that book
any instant
bound

wind rise or fall

where to begin, or end. A breath describes another passage, that tugs. Or "point of view." Without us, it has no wave upon

I'm interrogated

taut by repetition of a cry:
gull plowing wind

Smart folio, as if a knot could lead to an agreement. Answer in the words of the interrogator, the same words, your words. Ap-pearance has nothing to do with it.

portrait
of a political extremist, showing
a note in his own hand

trained viewers to come, who will demand

you, lover, the disproven equation.

an art, or living exponent, reducing desire to "I want myself." Hunger, on the other hand, inhabits, sends its nakedness out. The distance between us collapses.

would despair at that long
seizure were it not

dissent

in the stone, in the wood, a bit
of graphite hidden in a rubber mat

book imposes incalculable requirements. My photograph condemns me, then returns to silver ore. Witnesses are lulled by the slow pace of a poem. They leave, thinking it done.

could not repeat

wheel ran him over

fast enough. Substitute
another pane, clear vantage
for his labor.

prototype of all deaths since, so easily reproduced. Turn a page of history, bury the axis. Keep turning. What's covert, what's censored? What's proven

Relative hunger
the pistons
extend waking up
and down the strand

each an eye
on one, one
on the mill.

The question of habitat undefined in and from thinking about making friends with a pulley. I lose a thought. A sea bird asks me what I'm writing. Another boy, another girl: how simply they give up their lives!

ceased laughing
and is happy

as were her troubling

, earned tranquililty

never the moment, but its qualities end. Which are each of us. Find the thread from which she is suspended. Nevertheless, she is painting a dark blue, a floral, and will die.

precarnate
rush which underlies
deflates a thought

failing to compose
the time a tern a second
chases

The wish to return has no duration, no terminus.

, stoked,
what to do with
succulent, all
provocation

, revved
and practice being seen
a'dancin'.

At the end of the story she's a teen. A cure found, she clipped off the little plastic legs. Everyone saw her, mostly the men, but didn't notice. They swelled to fill their seats, to fit the pattern of the upholstery, and bled.

By race,
that is a glottal
stricture in a man's
calling, intuit

centuries,
churn over me.

divides what you can count on over cutting you. Without rest. Evidence in bricks and magic dolls accumulates, evaporates and grows heavy in all. The difference do not want to be the same. Clothed

The traffic, going 60,
other side of the park, tree
top level, glass
bell ringing:

When I returned, years later, I found the same random patterns there on the wall. Exact. Yet I could no longer imagine them depicting women's bodies, beckoning, coupling with men.

We sit, talk
in a circle.

Above our heads, another, and
above that, heat forms yet
another, the end points of the arc
extended, reach, at last

know our work
will not be finished.

figure of the minuet. Paths in the dark green wood are worn, intricately covered, and worn again in others' ways. It is dusk – you must look closely. See how your foot on the springing earth

The westerly pull, the known
fields yellowing

so like a dark
cape, and in

my shadow
my daughter
dances.

penniless, my familiar suddenly before me. Nor have these fears aged. I remain distant from this kernel, which lives in my belly, my throat and writing hand. What was the lesson? Memory serves like the knife, scraping away

Gil's hand so
shook when he lifted

the liquid

table, causing
it to tremble more.

flaws are mine in my eyes magnified as through the eyes of another. This is how I am counted. The man the clay wed, bruise the clay. Considerate and inflict.

Easy. Too
is what and what
is green, a word mean?

enter
there,
nor

Meaning is swift, then gone.

monotonous
accomplishment. Two

women, walking, agents
of cadence

of each step
into the elapsed
season.

If they don't know their own minds, how am I to give it to you? Say a cheek brushes on a sleeve: what is given, and what taken? An armature, a mannequin, this beautiful thing infuriates me!

A crew
procedures us

to port

confident the ropes,
the very screws, fitted

whole thought to acted

Concede, to get it down, its metaphor. The place in between, where poetry occurs. This indirection celebrates agreement among us. More than that, say, a straight line, or plumb to a wall, unerect

back

sitting
across, one from
the other, a tension, as if
unexpected, the report
of a spoon on

a pact

let into my life," myself unaware that there is entry or prohibition. Talk is idle. It is the difference between what I have been taught, and what I might learn. So evil, or what we now call

drinking
red wine

the skyline like a toy, and over it, a ceiling of clouds, parted, from which I or some other look. Masquerading as the dead, a music without reference. Standing here on the ledge, I imagine and resist the increments of change. But my victories are only

Each nature
mines on the mud road into town

scattered petals, like a blood
canticle.

Without bias, nature yields rhetoric. Writers, musicians, none to be seen.

Question the horse with its belly out. Have you ever heard such a fantastic story?

by that car or by
the driver himself, fat
chance

to get even,
passing him, turning, keeping
up.

Did I mention the breadth of the street, made white, emptied by the light and heat? Sunday. Wearing Sunday clothes. Pity issues, little more, tucked under viscera. Convenience

to themselves, the aging son
particularly, sullen
holiday. "Queer

white people
shoot and run

Attending, too few handles on the action. An utterance: of the son, it is humility and respect. But of the parent, torpor giving rise to crime.

The several languages, in passing
over, douse and evaporate

likeness. Swelling

smarts "to the bones

Languid punning, ambiguous heat. The wave penetrate, its inaudible take your substance for meat. The operations of a mouth, the gestures, apparently at play elude. Finger tip lift a drop of water to the raw

She is waiting
for him.

Due to the storms, tenacity supercedes regular growth. They went indoors and hardly left for several days. Through the grapevine fell between them before the road reopened.

more feral
that'd take a name
and bite

policy-making a quality car, or the ore to smelt for one. Displaced the men and squirrels. Rewrite intent, and the collapse of native messengers, complicated extricacy. Such short memories!

have
twelve
cents,
Sir?

and the sandwich
in my pocket

making poems. My bench, one that's empty, then their benches. The taste of cheese and mustard still in my mouth, although the day, cool and green, these sleeping men might share.

other where
in the house, forcing his head
under
hearing

at 50 yards, an animal
whelp. The boy

rationale to accommodate that residue. Understanding fear is not fear. One, one hundred steps, the trail the dragged weight makes. Decided to end

beginning
the beginning
of the book

What is the best thing to do *now*? The book is looking forward, with empty hands, toward you. It is grounded in the failure to begin. Death is little, dying large.

has clawed
a sly

medallion, slick
w/blood

himself. A votive candle. A glance. His magisterial presence reduced to a spasm, the white droplet flowering in the opaque red.

her husband

how they
part a tacit

pat
to pick it up
later

Holding the short blade. To the man's throat. In the field of battle he does not need. To look. Toward the dais. To gain the eye of the prince. The veins on his wrist and hand. Standing taut.

girl

crying

at all the world's companionship
by one

diminished

concerned with beginnings to stumble on the breach. When the applause died down, a praying mantis handed me the microphone. "None of you has read a word," I told the crowd. "God damn the book!"

beasts, chained, raging
silhouetted wood
the last
of winter's hold

diminished. Abraded. What will grow from, or does she pucker at the wound? And what else is prayer? A clasping of

constant
hissing
chrome and hard, black rubber

a sharp
account

Dear Charles
the desert citrus
grove, the dome

of far and bright

What is wasted becomes religion. Ice in the heights, and the deaf one there, to pure tonic bound. Fear the lyric, not audition. Take you out and you go on.

A place released,
a wooded fen in early
ever woodpiper, tufts

of grass to hop
the unsteady

metaphor

Do I have to explain everything to you? Now, leave me alone.

my body
strange, thin
my voice

She can see that it is bruised, but still she will apply the needle. Nod toward the little creek running in the past. The blue myosote

electric
hum

substation
by the tall
trees

that you inhabit and constantly address are not your body. It it. It's failure, your shame.

grazing the uncertain
reality
of my flank

An empty
hour,
        another

students, they discussed the potential of psychedelics. Sitting, thoughtless, alive, the unnatural, the unyielding, posture. Compelled to denial to live, desiring. To return.

that remains:
the two girls' foot
steps, running

in the hall, nearer
and away, nearer

this poem, the notebook open on the bed where you might find it. One is one alone, is one among others. However it is phrased, it is a question.

forgotten
where to go what
comes next

pacing

not angry!"

Between the two of them, a third, the two of them. I'm never really sure *what* I feel. I make a fist, raise my voice. I'm such a bad actor!"

of the muscle, knotted
rope, he drags

obsessively as to himself

notice, all of us,

the other foot. All together now pretending, ward it off. Retreat to I am whole. There are words for the one worse off. Words signifying feelings retrieve

makeshift
surviving, have

chosen
this neighborhood to winter

in: suddenly
filling a block of trees

crows

Less a matter of choice than of adaptation, foresight than tenacity. If you don't think it real, is it still a dream? And if not, then what is it? And which is more frightening?

old friends.

Which one is speaking
and which listening?

Grace not sought, not avoided.

at the
ebb, all
out

but, to say "no"
when asked, again
"no."

Her stare is meant to fix an expectation. Security in stone, encase our tiny drama. At its edge no other bone and muscle. Patiently prying in the darkening

reach

How a blade of silver
delights!

What are you looking for? Setting – as on a trip? – or as in traps? – I never tire of that fare. A memory. What further proof that you are eating yourself.

She is
an artist

eye and hand

no longer mine, but hers,
my child.

If I have written a line, it has become unknown to me.

Poems from *The Form of Our Uncertainty*

edited by Kristen Gallagher

Chax Press / handwritten press

2001

SOLIDARITY

"How when I put up my antennae
the world's buzz oer
wells not deep enough
to hold the dead I

back t back off. My
creed's argument, n's caused
fr mete survival — wot
good's a corpse. s's no

r solvent at sick
victim shit, ooze a gut
whine's bord, all flatulent.
Na. Carve it up. Come

pretty pretty progress m
eater limits, my back yard
aroses ground an ear
me out. I i i've gotta

say sun'n hell t boast
a cracker shot, suck, indio
principalis piss — yg
step on a few roaches

d'we (bite) are the world
(chew) homily d spite h big
pichchur n'a sea's sparkly
mirror (swallow) aw (spit) sa

flaw. I tire f certain t't
out. T'ang cod of gadda sod
patch, moan backyard n homo
neurotic wife and kid to high

dense eke a secret life.
Men titled end serve it
's outside the calculation period.
Now. Workin' I due f'you?

HEAVEN

From the park
to the parting of the waters

one ball of tinfoil
one avocado
three sticks of gum

the small leaves of a fiddle
fern feathering and evenly spaced

t'endure
common inhumanity and neglect
t tier n tier yr

step measuring light a gain
strew holiness strain
sa frosted window
less aperture

'sall around us, the light, ever
she finds everly
dust magnified t'hit n ent her
up here eh among d
d zzi glorious err t terror

atop a tower

swats me, runs up behind
n hits me on
th head w a baseball
flutter determination
walking
smell of rain,
staying in the rain

am
a thing most solid, to myself
counting
foot
fall twenty forty sixty breath um ar
t'beats

b step a break-
fast (toast, jelly, cof

was it Monday, St Peter's,
meal on Tuesday (holds
body and soul
two

dollars tend
r pass n'out t'be

vulnerable, hungry, deprived
of sleep a wking
dream

a' millenial flight, in
the upper air a door
wraith th there y
see! ch born n unborn
waving fore t wrd m
welcome, pulled
up and in co
hearing call — a constant ring
ing heaven's annular core

us among the missing — ha! — a fool
t'take their money, lie

abed thr
shelter how
thll pull y'in m'

arm's s started t'tingle II
get arrest bray
thing coming shallow w
the weather bet
b bettter het th
fourth street bridge
early, get
a ledge up

bets a doorway

step pace pr count ten
leven thirdteen four phase sun

light sharp to clouded sharp
cold to stifling
heat, winds cloud's

evanescent passage or the earth'
s a system so bright

I cannot
see myself I am more likely
my shadow

here, in Heaven m
m multiple n no more
use for a name

Note: "HEAVEN" was commissioned by Glenn Holsten of Philadelphia's WHYY TV, as part of the "Poets and Places" series. The place, in this case, is the Benjamin Frankling bridge, a 20's ear suspension bridge, a baroque celebration of industry and human achievement, incorporating the only means by which one can walk from Philadelphia to Camden, New Jersey. Performed, "HEAVEN" is monologue, a composite of several shelter residents who I have known over the years.

ON LEARNING OF THE DEATH OF A POET

For Daniel Davidson

What I cannot do to music
and removed, having listened
without hearing, to fail and fail

t'attribute rs t'dying s
remedy deny mine
n y passage so accurately

distor ted or ment, I lack
brtly demonstrated. Y cleave
th flaw b lie b art m

pale neglect, I cannot
soften bread in salt
I lone wndr r, gone.

Child, aye, n stumble up
on awe soliloquy ea diminishes
us. Wr

tng me, all unprepared, n
echo stain, unchanged,
unchanging, laugh it

lost imaginary, could
escape yr interpreter, evade
the harrowing metaphor. G

wch y grant.

THIRST

for Rick Webb

trip nminute's
digital ghost whips
air in the hollow

hiding her face as she runs, or was
that a fabric moving without

range, every inch
of skin, each muscle and the soft
function

moth
ing room to room undetected
and to myself

nearly strange.
Interrupt n nightly rope a tense immobile
twist prohibited

d light inhabitant craves
fleet gimme checks
s somnolent inhibitor walking
among a self strong and ragged.

Thirst denied, addiction's
ironic pass-a-hand/face
at the glass

to solvents fumes deeply
abandoned. F'ew
look at it morren once

it crumbles, it teases, it
chids and punishes
at the shimmering brook, afraid

with bleach and breath's revival
unacquainted
to take a step

conceived, rehearsed, debated,
weighed, disputed
withheld

against a wall
where there is no

touches myself, and feels
me touching
and decides
there can be no purpose

enjoying bodily
dusted interminable thinking

& spittle.

SKUNK

Of detritus
up and counting,
so'm to poetry: midst and apart
my generation.

Ode tavoy
t creatures underground
mix form weaning
the sweet, sweet

apoplect g chance semantic
account. Rhyme
me out. Flew
days catched

behind me, breathing
hard. Bits
of plan swarm
short of relic:

my behavior isn't noticed.
What fun! Look
how they mate!
World to tickertape

round the big
bend, atoms exhaled.
Three, for the most part,
words per line

sums a stanza
'
s premium p form
a ask Alice
I think she'll

lam on memory.
Consider
the shape of the back of the
head, its ascent

through candle flame,
and while you're
aroused a prick
to juice it

up your autobiography.
This, this poem perhaps, this
is your first
hand to stroke

a thorough, sensual
grip a little woman bound.
Shit. Git
all over the rug

n titer pussles
average pone. Where's the out
a dream a child a lull

in a bush arms
promised? When yr
dead the cells
g'on gunk

a skunk's first
philosophical muse.
Chells lk chells splattered
n spread abt

the floor shiny
dotted mercury, a mess
a geture cdn't
get amidst.

THE CHEESE STANDS ALONE

The farmer the the naked and scarred
acquisitive hook resists the insinuation

of the word that planted sprouts a myth
that threshed and tied a net to trap him, grunts.

Heigh! Ho! The bankers pinch the pink,
Old Man, on your Wife's cheek and scuff

your seed up two per cent, up two per sent
the soil that you also owe somebody, groans.

Time out! Time out! The pinwheel skull
the hot hot fi of silver silver phosphor

where your eyes go haywire takes
the dog takes the cat down a windmill's

pretty patch and steeple, see the people
out to lynch a commie or a Jew. Art you

the derry-oh, the fink, the snitch, the one
betrayed the bitch, the child, the cow, her dowry

of cheese?

POEM, FOR WILLA

Were it told, my
maple-girl, my paper-warm
October girl, the beach
ahead of us would speak our name as one, a sound
that only ancient water churning
ancient gravel utters

with authority. Our storied
origin in seed and metaphor
perplexes yet, and yet demands
the question and its tensions be
relinquished, love, how

chrysanthemums purple, mantises
their foam and futures know how to make.

BY GIL OTT AND JULIA BLUMENREICH

This sequence of thirteen poems was written collaboratively in 1985. Passing the notebook back and forth over a period of weeks, it was a way we came to know each other

Poem #1

Call on
the pleasure of that small disturbance
no one

two

activate

Poem #2

stone sculptures
carved outside
the transit stop

in relief
"...the deepest station in the city."

looking down, she's dizzy;
and up, the worker's reach

Poem #3

Plant whose
virtues have not
yet been discovered -
one particular,
watching over

the hold on
the home free
the away where

indigenous lessons
pause over
cornflower
sky, the inside of a petal
least of all separate -
how tallness happens

Poem #4

subject to tableau
stands thus, are it contra blue
since the subject's

more the soundtrack. They dance,
we dance. Wind
that will bring rain.

Poem #5

The vane senses
for instance we
were nearly up in

Mercury sweeping the drapes
aside
happened happened happened

first notation: the house shifts

Poem #6

among houses, each

form on leaving the familiar

Poem #7

intervene, two hands to disassemble
enterprise itself. Care and uninstructed

sense to me. My beautiful friend arrives
in sumac, the scent of her parts

to move on one diagram
deprived of commensurate time.

I'm content. Four steps
confound a reel

suggests a window, or fragment
still in the midst you'd see

Poem #8

numeric memory the one,
two, the more and

All is essential
or restrictive, hours'
unadornment aggregates from
there we discern *such*
a tiny every,
underfoot

is planning and is elevating
"voices like golden trumpets"

recal while they begin,
not a buzz assembles
our misses. One seize
over another one hand
over do onto

Poem #9

reach
along   or is it
your

                                             game
                                             violates
skin's equilibrium, an eco-
abstract as a third who talks
in phases. One of us
                    to myself
                    around, reaching

under no
disserence

Poem #10

preposition as of description
into words   =   script
                    long tresses
                    a man's belt wraps
some multi-colored bobbins assuage
a table from a cable spool

latitude (lass) as other's arms
round out length to
perpendicular easy dimensions
R&R (you & I reading &) or
have equal
grow up to trees

a piece of paper lies level
if or — tosses until
stops transferred

Poem #11

As you age, a table
companioned. You on the vertical, I'm flat,
a paper record we
were. What more?

have no advice. She dreams her
blue and yellow dirndl spinning.

Poem #12

theory of differences
don't watch him going to prison

or the wind up her skirt, even
grammar the same. Your inventions

not my waddle though there've been times
at table
we've gone driving.

Two, animal
legs, two hands.
Make work.

Poem #13

Chronologically:
stood still at the edge of the field
was observed, perhaps
then broke
the law
omits passion and cause. Certain
lamentation from a select
you, enough to numb
haste. Couldn't get
out if I tried. The blads
of grass
cut me, damn poetry.

Pact

Singing Horse Press

2002

KEDARDO

Can you see the moon from your window? First you must turn off the electric light, and then lean close to the glass. But even that is not enough. You have to put on your slippers and robe and walk downstairs and out, further out through the tall grass in the back to get away from the utility pole and its buzzing lamp.

Still further out. The dew has not yet settled, and you can feel the field's uneven surface through your thin footwear. This is important. As you head toward the canebrake silhouetted black against that deeper, unknown black, you feel yourself strangely distinct from your surroundings. Not the pads of your feet, but the serial impression made on them by stick, stem, stone, is the only thing attaching you to the earth. The seat of your perceptions sits so high on your shoulders you can subtract its distance from the ground in calculating the range of the intermittently plausible leap a man could make

> one late spring night
> up to the moon. A man
> may imagine full wonderful

acts based in the joyous ratiocinations of the child he remains throughout life toward the grown-up he is forever becoming, acts of daring, strength and agility, spiritual elevation, compassion, intellect, platonic love, or moral fortitude. It is easy for a child to impress himself, but an adult learns to excuse or postpone.

Are you listening? Who is that pest continually batting at your attention? How is it that he reaches up from behind, where you can't see him, and pinches you between the legs? Where does he come from, where does he go, and why does he torment only you?

A popular figure at the traveling circuses of the island state of Dominica, Kedardo's role is to distract members of the audience from the performance. Did I say he is popular? Well, he is universally detested. The contortionist, who makes her entrance into the center ring in a ten-liter fish tank carried by two attendants, and who then unfolds limb by limb from the tiny glass box, adamantly denies any knowledge of him. He is filthy. As the Gran Señor, Master of Ceremonies, grandiloquates, directing our attention to the trapeze, a shriek comes from the stands. It cannot interrupt the Señor, but from that vibrating honker of a frantic woman (preferably one of notable heft and dignity) waves of disturbance ripple aggressively through the crowd. Men stamp their feet, women squeal and blush, children panic. Kedardo, however, is never seen.

I saw him once, but only with the assistance of an optical procedure which enables one to see those aspects of the human form normally hidden from the eye. This rare glimpse supplemented the many manual inspections a man (or woman, for that matter) makes daily. I can report that Dardo is indeed small and puerile in appearance, a fact oft contradicted in my hopes and his effect. It would appear that his physique has developed irregularly, his legs prominent while his upper parts remain hidden. These legs he clothes in lurid purple breeches of an extruded, hairy fabric, which stretches or compresses to accommodate Dardo's elastic requirements. Perhaps he is ashamed of his pranks. Why else would he favor the dark and upper reaches of the world? In appearance, Kedardo is a disappointment. In fact, his only skill the insult, the petard, the ambush.

But will you not confirm that a person's capacity for faith, which alone distinguishes humanity from the rest of the planetary crowd, issues from these very interruptions and irritants? So did Moses, a Prince of Egypt, have his faith restored. Had not Pharaoh ordered the execution of the Hebrew firstborn, thereby rending the succession of the faith, the baby would not have been trusted to the river's course, the sequence set in motion whereby fealty and faith were then and have been ever since contested. Consider the canebrake at the Nile's edge, a border, if you will, between habitable and uninhabitable, between order and chaos, the lovely servant girl those rushes parting with her trembling hands, hands which remember the way the Pharaoh himself so skillfully, so firmly parted her own knees the night before, to find a miracle, a babe afloat in that secluded, watery way. The girl is struck dumb by the coincidence of pink, warm and wrinkled things, her faithful tongue extended as to meet them.

Just a story, perhaps, but into the interstices of subject predicate agreement the marvelous would like to insert a blade. To pry. Song is a form of travel, no here, no there, the body, song's instrument, continually rejoined. I went out on a moonlit night, heigh, ho, I never did return. I packed eventuality in a little checkered case, and on the way I lost it.

Like any powers, Dardo's are his only insofar ceded. Music's doubt, anticipation's patience, choice's elation, definition's fear. There's no getting away from him, yet here he is, fascinated by the caged rodent on his go-round. He leans his elbows on the table and watches for hours. Who could resist the child-like appeal of one so simply amused? Contingent upon rupture. Approach and find yourself alone, Dardo vanished. Speak to him and call yourself a fool.

I would not want to exaggerate Kedardo's prowess. Ubiquitous, perhaps, but from, say, a lunar vantage, less than insignificant. The moon's surface is cold and airless, and above all, pristine. Only imagination has ever walked here, and here it throngs, doubtless loosed by the storied and treasured moon dust which lies several inches deep upon the surface. Here are the persistence of a strong and gentle cock, the straight-eyed compliance of the dove, the stalker, the crowded cattle car, falling, imposture confidence unmasked. Here, too, is Dardo, nobody, nothing, not.

EVIDENCE

Because I am vulnerable when I sleep, I bundle and tie the evidence with a heavy string and hang it inside the chimney from the flue. Without my leg, I can't get around like I used to, but when I do, is often up through the chimney passage I go. This version of freedom is easiest to manage, fronting as it does directly on cold, starry night. I've been too trusting, and too often cheated in my life. When I was young I indulged in the common fantasy of free will. I traveled, and adapted my trade to local opportunity. In one town I was a cook, in a larger city I delivered the mail, and so on. In a small town in Puget a fisherman let me live on his boat while I helped him winter in, paint and repair, mend nets, that sort of thing. I had a tiny wood burner to keep me warm, and nights bundled in a sleeping bag I'd stare at those orange coals and rock with the water. The water is huge, heavy and indifferent. When the fisherman's daughter came to see me one night, and then began to visit regularly, I never asked her mind. Her body was stocky and familiar, like an armchair, a convenience. The skin covering her squarish face was taut, though not necessarily young, and despite her general lack of expression, intricately etched. I could see she was troubled, but I did not have the patience. I left that place without a word to anyone. Everyone, I have learned, keeps secrets in plain view, and we all, by some unspoken contract and fearing our own exposure, agree to overlook. Perhaps you think this sounds utopian. You have no imagination. When I talk about my experiences under water, you call them fiction. Your reliance on entertainment is debilitating. Do you find my desperation diverting? When I describe that first moment of panic, having entered the water and then feeling the weight pushing down on my shoulders, what do you call that pale little twinge that you feel in your gut? And since you don't believe in your own experiences, you can't accept the calm which comes over me when I stop resisting and finally inhale.

So it is for your sake that I began collecting the photographs and letters, testimony, bruises, documented lies and half-truths, clippings, paraphernalia and talismans that are my evidence. Here is a letter, two, three, another, a bundle of letters from my attorneys, first from Simon Walt, who, I now see, led me on during that first critical year following the accident and surgery, and then from Brian Karp, who continues to represent me, even though he has done little to advance my case. He loves to say to me: "An addiction is an addiction. You find a way out, or you don't. No half solutions." Here are some fragments of teeth. A recurring dream. The doorway is dark, like a highway rushing toward me in the rain. I've waited here before. Is this my street? I feel no more familiar with its broken row-houses, or even the one light at the window two houses up, always on, but wait with an increasing anxiety which, with each visit, I gradually come to anticipate and know, and so surpass my strangeness. Here are two nails. Hold them in the palm of your hand forever.

Catching the light, an amulet, a silver death's head, a pact made over a bottle of cheap wine. A feeling lasts a very short time. After that, you can never be yourself. I will not say his name betrayed me. I have proof of it, here. The light comes down the West Virginia foothills like a messenger of God where we don't need any god.

Kick back. Prepare a rustic camp with our machines at the heart. Freed of women have a tough and silent agreement. Cut the ground by swastika, bite, chew, out of my delirium. Cut the evidence the sun is setting. Here is a crutch. I've made shelter on the side of a hill, from a blue plastic tarp thrown over a motorcycle, boots for a pillow. Now it's difficult to cross the room. A chair is in the way, a tile is loose, the water is boiling for instant soup. There are more types of pain than of tenderness. Or rather, pain is the tenderness once shown me by a man. He took my incapacity for his own. Try to forget out of need that he is a man, or that I am one. He lifted my right leg and placed it over the left, then turned the two together so that I gently rolled onto my back. He looked at my face, and he brushed the dirt from it. He straightened my shoulders, then, returning to the damaged leg lifted it again and bent it to my chest, pushing and flexing, reintroducing the flow of blood. Share strength, impart confidence, take them away. Here is evidence of my thirst. An x-ray. An ache at every joint.

Why are you still here? You force me to grit my teeth, get up and show you the door. Why can't you simply find it yourself? You must realize that you are on your own. How are arrangements made, for travel, lodging, companionship, in a foreign country, in an unknown language? You pretend to know things you don't. It's the surface of things that's exotic. Believe me, decay is mundane. The sidewalks are narrow, there's a milk-colored stink running in the gutter. Get closer still. Heat and thirst. Sharp sunlight shatters off in several directions, but not in all, driven and inhibited by the sound of unrestrained engines. You crawl through the marketplace in the belief that commerce will somehow sustain you, and you are confronted by the corpse of a crow. Returning to your room, you sense that someone has gone through your things. But I would rather talk about myself. I am the one who has violated your privacy. Here are thirteen views of the city, all from the air. What looks like concrete and glass is actually a flow, a flower, a surge of dying that sparkles and pushes at its banks. The flood rushes out over the clay plain and where it touches a new palm begins. The flesh of it is unseasoned. It is sensitive to the least touch. Here is the book that tells of it. It is the book of my body. There is no other book.

PRSPHNE

My girl is over there.

Here in this narrow steel box are my poems. The box is my belly.

Every day I leave what little I know for the greater uncertainty of getting by. I have neither trust nor memory.

When my girl dances she dissembles. The curve of her upper arm; the pull of flesh over her ribs.

Woman — as we have come to be known — does not correspond to the world. Woman is interior.

A slight resistance in the armature, then the gears' teeth settle and mesh.

> What is this season? The red-
> tailed anchorite has flown, but who
> could blame him? Now the coals,
> which also once were red, are cooling.
> Now the scent has thinned where once
> she tread.

Where my body leaves off, and hers begins.

The throbbing pain in my right foot, which comes and goes whether I am walking or at rest. The mundane destination. I continue walking, right, mute, right, mute, mechanical shifting of the hips.

Forgetting begins where absence begins. The first frost at dawn. The beautiful pattern climbing the blade.

A poem is written this same way: the unknowable pushing its way into the unknown.

> Sharp, coarse descriptor.
> Tiny irritant. I have made
> a promise I must daily
> reinforce. Every
> insect, every dying weed
> enjoys a laugh
> at my expense.

Over there. A drop of blood blossoms on hitting water. Doubt consumes me.

I don't know what I'm doing. Motion of a grinding wheel at work. The slightest wisp of breeze distracts me. My girl's sweet breath!

Over there. She is prey to demons, rapists, stalkers. Worse: she is not.

As she has come out of me, I dissolve in my imagining of my lost girl. All around me the shrieking of machines. I cannot stop my ears.

I cannot — will not — introduce any new element into the story. I may hopelessly wander the past or future, but I cannot tolerate the present.

I, I, I. I am so tired of myself. Yet I continue. Perhaps my girl requires a vessel.

> Pare, and pare, and harvest
> tears. Sow fat and boil
> complacency and wake
> broken in the morning.
>
> If only I knew now what I know
> now I could believe
> in my girl's absence, her return.

What is there in the dirt, the cold air and sun that is not myself, alone?

At night, a riot of constellations. Insomniac, I ceaselessly inspect each cuticle, hairline, every pore and crease of my body, looking for the bruise that will begin my girl's story.

TUNNEL

Again, night is falling. How can I tell? The birds begin to act up, as now, at dusk. A little light still comes in at the crack in the hatch at the end of the tunnel. My husband left it like that when he went out two days ago.

The measurement of time occupies me. He could return at any moment, and I must be ready to receive him. This is quite difficult, in the dark, in this tunnel. My clothes are soiled with mud at the slightest movement. The preparation of meals, which usually gives me some pleasure, is cramped and driven only by hunger. Of course, all of this is made worse by my condition.

My husband is a good man, a hard worker who cares for me. He would not be done for so long with-out reason. He helped dig this tunnel with the other men, before so many of them fled. We'd all known that the war would eventually come to our settlement, but our preparations, the digging of tunnels and laying in of stores, advanced so slowly. We had little to spare. So when the smell of fighting came — and it did not come without warning — the houses around us gradually emptied.

My husband and I did not leave, due, I suspect, to my weakness. I had anticipated leaving, packing a small amount of food, a blanket, setting these by the door, but when he noticed this he declared we would be staying. He called the others cowards, but I saw that he, too, was afraid.

I am not afraid. Mostly, I am saddened, to have put the two of us in harm's way. When the first of the combatants came up from the river bank and spread out through the empty streets, my husband spoke to them. It was brave of him to do so, but they did not see him as a threat. They were in retreat, they said, warning that a larger group would follow soon. They took the food and blanket I had packed. That evening, at dusk, as now, my husband and I entered this tunnel.

I call it a tunnel, but it has become much more to me. Before I was born, my parents were told by their doctor that I would be compromised. They could not know the exact nature of my problem, the unpredictable fevers, the dizziness and possessions, the periods of absolute stillness, neither sleep nor waking, when I would respond to no suggestion. While I suffer from no physical handicap, I have lived my entire 23 years within the boundaries of our settlement, mostly inside my parents' house, or, when we married five years ago, my husband's. So I am accustomed to confinement.

It is a tunnel, but then, a tunnel must lead somewhere. At this end, near the hatch, it is narrow, but further down it grows broader, wide enough to hold twenty people. Alone, I am all twenty of us. In our collective hunger, we often act as one. Naturally, this deprivation wears on our patience, and we sometimes act violently, without warning, against one of our number. This behavior frightens my husband. After one particularly violent incident, which flared against a young woman a few days ago and as quickly subsided, he began talking to me as if I weren't here. He tore his shirt to bandage my arm, which I had hurt in the fight, and then left to see if any medical supplies remained in the clinic near our house. The trip should not have taken more than an hour or two.

But, as I have said, a tunnel is a passage. I have not wasted my time in waiting, but have examined this place thoroughly. Since its beginning, it has begun to show signs of its illness. The walls themselves secrete a sticky fluid which collects in puddles. These are very difficult to avoid as I crawl in the darkness toward the awakening I know will come.

I cannot underestimate the importance of this occupation. At the far end of the tunnel, I have seen a certain worm, which, in the past, I have caught, mixed with cooked rice, and eaten. The feeling is gone from my right hand where the bandage is saturated with blood, and with my left alone I have trouble holding onto these worms. Yet I try incessantly, crawling into the dark, and crawling back. I have been at it the entire day. Of every two I catch, I save one for the husband. I have kept his dinner pot full, and the mat on which he sleeps rolled up on the narrow shelf of dirt beside my own.

DEAR R

I've just gotten up from a dreadful, long afternoon sleep. You weren't in it — no one was, for that matter, not even me. Fear is always induced by some preconscious guess, a collision. The solid wall, or floor, or chair, gives way, is penetrable, and we go inside.

You'll remember the letter I received from M last summer. It created a misunderstanding between us because I wouldn't tell you what it said. We'd been isolated there at the lake for over a week, so I guess you felt entitled. And of course you knew M far better than I did. I finally dismissed the issue by saying M would be there with us a few days later, and she could tell you herself what she'd written. You really should have let the issue drop, but you wouldn't. We didn't talk after that for a full day. Anyway, this dream I just had — or lack of dream, I should say — has made me want to tell you about that letter.

Sleep, for me (and I'm sure I'm not unique in this), has become the only reliable escape. Dreams don't exist until you recall them, and I've been trying to discipline myself to recall them favorably. You see, our real lives are deeply private and uncertain. Sometimes all we've got is the will. This goes for everything, not just dreams, but we're trained early on to accept the social contract, which is a waking, constructed reality.

I'm sorry this seems so involved. It is important, urgent, now. I haven't seen M since last summer, and she stopped writing to me some months back. Can you say where she is?

I am troubled by the image of an all-absorbing darkness that underlies whatever we see or touch. It is not constantly before me, and often even gives me some warning before appearing, but it is always horrifying. It can be simple: I'm reading a book and the pages corrode, or watching a bird on a wire and see its feathers and flesh gray and slough off leaving a little crackling toy which evaporates. These are short warnings. Usually, my perception addles as I grow momentarily and inexplicably tired, then I become aware that the condition of the earth and everything around me is thoroughly saturated. The world is exhausted at all surfaces.

Now that I'm writing to you about this, I realize that the landscape of this afternoon's sleep was the lake we visited last year. You'll remember that the water almost completely surrounded our cottage, which sat out on a little promontory. The house is gone. There is a loud, oppressive rumbling from beyond the trees on all sides. Although it is daylight, there are stars, but they are dark stars, and they are not so high in the sky, like stones pinned up there, as if the limits of the sky itself had descended.

This scene is my body. It is your body, also alone. The lake is black and absolutely still. Somewhere in my skull blunt puncture sounds, at random, rifle shots aimed at no particular target. I flinch — that's what wakes me — and concentric circles inch out from a point in the perfect lake.

This is the same image M described to me in her letter. This disturbs me most of all. The obvious question, to me, is whether or not she planted it here, today, to throw me off or lead me on. I can't know what lines she's crossed, or what kind of trouble she might be in.

M and I had been corresponding for over a year about what we called sensory flaw and everyday illusion. To her, it was top secret; I think she was hoping it would develop into the core of a novel or some other writing. It was a pretty simple idea: we'd each look for instances of perceptual gaps, moments when things don't quite add up, like the appearance of two suns in the sky after a rough storm, or a missing reflection in a mirror. We'd write to each other about them. I tended to treat the project taxonomically, expecting to find patterns, categories, that sort of thing. But for M each flaw was pure. She wanted to penetrate the least fissure. Since these phenomena tend to be ephemeral, she developed a kind of meditation based on sensory deprivation that extended their moment. This takes an incredible level of concentration. If you can do it long enough, the flaw transmogrifies, reveals more of itself, but if you fail, it becomes an increment of terror, a little grain that rubs you constantly.

At the time I received that letter from her last year, M was on the verge of her first breakthrough. She and I had been arguing a bit through the mail, because I only saw her becoming morose and paranoid with it. She'd given up her writing career. She'd begun talking incessantly about the potential for moving what she called "metaphysically significant objects" across the sensory border. By her description, these included things like razors, calipers, guns. Strangely, everyone around her, yourself included, was unaware of her obsessions. I was the only one who knew what she was up to. And while it all excited me, I genuinely feared for her safety. My only argument was that I couldn't' see what use there could be in it. Of course, she didn't buy that, and I think from that time she wasn't completely open with me.

M and I never discussed the correspondence when we were together. Maybe you didn't notice the change in her when she arrived at the lake. I saw a slight twitch around her eyes, and there was a sluggishness to her movements. I didn't say anything. I was glad to be relieved of our letter-writing.

Maybe this doesn't seem so dangerous to you. I'd welcome your assurances, especially if you can tell me M's whereabouts, anything. Since I've lost touch with her I sometimes find myself staring, at a curtain moving at an open window, or at a dust mote across the floor. It's not M who is there — nobody's there, absolutely — but my own absence. Certain objects turn up missing, like a small knife last month, or a scissor. And each of my small failures is like a finger, a foot, some part of my body cut from me.

I hope you can forgive me. Please write soon.

ACADEMY

Love. My love is small as a bat. Perhaps a bit larger: a winged flap folding over on itself. A black handkerchief. An admission.

Unfold the flap it is starry and black. It is limitless. The opening to that place advances and contracts. A few drops, clear and precious, enter there and become fixed. Love leads me to understand that this is not a place, and it is gone.

I hold my love secret against the others, yet it is a secret commonly held. We turn out each morning, a yeasty aggregate, hungry. Having slept several to a bed, each longs for another out of reach, concocting a self which pushes and bruises, suppressing the discovery each thinks is his alone.

Who has the authority to catch and tell, and who to set the rules? Billy was caught needling in the closet. He was a wee wee. He ruddy all down the hall, in front of us all. Master Hastings following fiercely. I can say I don't. That's easy and true. Yet I do.

We wake up each morning over coffee and the acrid smell of new leather. This being the busy season, the tanning process goes all day and night. Each boy gets one hard roll: plain, cheese, or lingonberry. For this we are expected to work all morning, right up to the first class. After that, there are meat sandwiches and beer, followed by more studies, and athletics.

My favorite is soccer, a free form brand for which we make our own rules. The body is the purest poetry. All of us dressed in silk, in a line, our arms twined and many of us near big enough to show little breasts. This supple march proceeds towards its goal. Perhaps it gets a little rough; that only adds to the effect. When I am in the line, my hips pushed next to Jason's, or Malik's, the full bulk of the moment penetrates me, and I am lost to the team.

Even after the sun has gone and the cold air sets in, the excitement remains and seeks the little slit between our thighs. Were we without supervision, we would play into the night, but Mr. Banda calls us in for showers. There, exposed before the others, I feel ashamed.

I feel despondent. It is as if I had lost someone dear to me. Why, when the night, which is just arrived to envelop each of us singly, calls my name, do I hold back? She who would know me thoroughly, and who would doubtless reveal a cavity commensurate with mine in imperfection, stands impassive now, back lit, just outside a screen door in an early autumn evening. It's an image I can't shake. I scrub my anus. I linger even after the others have left the shower. I want to cry.

"She" departed years ago. She was an essence I have missed and overcome. Still, if I take time and contemplate, I can see her naked, rising out of the still lake. Her eyes look directly at me. Her breasts and stomach are slick with water. I am the water sinking into her thatch and running between her thighs.

Freedom is just outside the academy grounds. I am complete in myself, and, although my leaving may be awkward and surreptitious, leave. I find, after all, that the academy has no guard, no fence or boundary. The wood at the frontier is actually thin and easily traversed. Only the encroaching cold meets me, my insufficient clothing.

Any road I find will do, leading to all other roads. I hitchhike. The cars are small and fast, the drivers younger and with no more destination than I. I choose who I will talk to. These drivers' faces frost, each succeeding each increasingly unworthy of trust. Pick at the edge of ice up like a scab, the set snarl of a kid at the wheel brandishing a demand for sex, a story, aimless.

The cold lets me preserve myself waiting for better circumstances. Exposure must be pursued gradually, yet evenly. What are the borders of the self?

Moment by moment, they have to include all past and future, my eventual partner and offspring, my sure death and afterlife. These stalk me continually.

A moving interior, small capsule of light in the night, may be an unlikely place to meet that future in the form a another young man, yet it is there I meet Willow at the Edge of the Water. Like me, he is dislodged and vulnerable, and feels he will soon die. We are both at the mercy of movement. His skin is coarse, his reach wide enough to seem like shelter. He takes my name, and I listen to his every word. He closes my eyes with the tips of his fingers. He is gone.

In his place is a child running into my arms. Is this my little boy? I grow older as I raise him up and gather him close to me. He resists; I know what I must do. I reach up along his leg, along the seam I've seen that runs there, and find the handle of the zipper tucked beside his scrotum. He squeals wildly, and I am frightened, yet I pull, and the seam opens.

None can explain the violence of daily human relations. My boy looks at me with hatred and resignation, his face shriveling. When I drop him on the ground at my feet, another leg appears from the wound in his thigh. I step back. That leg is broken, with bone visible beneath gray flesh. More of the man inside emerges.

I turn and run. In my dream, the woods are lush in mid-spring. They are my external self. Sometime to come, I will return here seeking clues in the decay of hair and flesh that were to have been my mates. I will seek them in the minute crosshatch of twigs and rotting grass in my little clearing. There, near the house of my Master, I will drink, too much for my little head and task. I will be a boor, and make unwel-

come advances toward those I seek in memory. Outcast, I will come to doubt the very honesty that will have taken me to that turn.
But I am speaking in the present. I am awake and it is winter, so I will level with you. There are moments, say when I am walking alone at night on a rural road, my boot steps crunching without weight in the new snow, that I am relieved of myself. My constant meditation, that I am a seed struggling toward the aurora, lapses. Then I am joined, multiple, frozen and aware of all things moving swiftly about and without me. Then I am without sex, or rather, my sex is determined, and I am wed.

My wife and I have an agreement. I waits like arsenic on the pantry shelf. Take it from the dark and shake it.

EMPATHY

The man with the monkey face is still sitting there, on the sideway seats by the door. Three stops since I got on, and he hasn't moved. He's like a lump of dough, his arms in his lap, submerged but fully alert. He hasn't looked anywhere but straight ahead, but I know he's watching me in his little periphery.

The city is familiar, something I don't really notice. If I did, I'd go crazy. I'm in this big metal box hurtling along at rooftop level. There is no more home out this way. Just a room, a place to be alone.

I can't get off the train until the monkey man has gotten off.

"The next three months should tell us," the doctor said. That's all he would say. Doctors are used to their patients' wanting to relate to them personally. They expect it. Knowledge, science, that's power, applied to my life or death. If I'd asked him to fuck me he probably wouldn't've been surprised. He couldn't care less. He's the doctor, and I'm just a teenage girl.

Young black dude, all in leather, nodding off.

$120 in the bank. Another fifty Joanne promised me. Angel gone two weeks to Baltimore, looking for work. No word yet. Mom dead over a year. My clothes. Mom's necklace. Food stamps. Joanne said I should apply for food stamps.

Angel of the big cock. Angel lounging on a bench in the park on a warm day. Why can't I just leave it off, the teasing and the back and forth? Angel told me I was psychic. My first time with him, I was so scared. But it was almost like *I* seduced *him*, got him to come to Joanne's place even before I had a place of my own. Knowing Joanne wouldn't be there.

Here comes Margaret Orthodox. My stop.

Sure I miss Angel. I miss my sister Paula, too. And I miss my paycheck from Mr. Ortiz. But Angel, he'll be back by the end of next week. Or at least call. I know.

Shit. The monkey guy looks like he's getting off here, too.

* * *

See how even now, long after the big house on the corner has been abandoned, neglected and finally demolished, the rubble piled here and there attracting vermin, and the field leveled, how this field is unable to return to its original field but is at once and at all times innocent and ashamed of its innocence, how in the heat of summer weed stalks stand determined against the sun, and the slightest breeze, the rarest young thing, raises a faint clatter among the dying leaves. It is this breeze which is our subject. Place holds tenuous dominion in the human mind. Subordinate to place are witness and, following that, judgment, upon which we attempt to build. Yet we build so little, and so poorly. The mind wanders. It will not be fixed. We follow, or better to say we believe something preceded us. Return is a fixed place in our minds. We are met with vast plains, unforgiving weather, meanness and famine. We are fools to anticipate reward. Remain at all times fixed upon the movement of the air, wed to the complaint of the dry leaves. Can this be done? And, doing this, would we see surcease the frequent plagues, of roaches, virus, idleness and crime? Here and away, my child, so long as there is flesh to feed the flesh, delusion will be entertained, and lacking that, crawl forth close to the ground, all one and alone.

* * *

It's not like cramps, you know, like menstrual. It's so fucking hard to talk to a male doctor. Nobody seems made right anymore. Everybody looks sick, riding by in the buses, standing around. No, it's more focused than cramps. A pain in one place. It isn't anything that Angel did. He's not that big anyway. Or that weird night in Mr. Ortiz's store, being there way after I usually left, and that guy out front flashing me through the glass door. That was all he did, but I didn't want to leave for awhile, by myself. No. Nobody's hit me or fucked me too hard. What is this? Does it hurt when I've got to take a shit. When I press here? Press here? How should I know? This doctor is totally unsexy. He's just unpleasant to be around. His breath is bad. Why did Joanne send me to this guy? I wonder how he touches her. I touch myself. Move my hand up and over my belly. The skin is smooth, the pain is like a cube. Smooth on the sides, sharp on the edges. Points. How guys, cheat, chicks tell lies. My little, fuzzy pain has eyes. I'm watching me. I hold me in my hand, dissolve, the sugar cube in water warm. My pain goes like a dog up the street in the dark. Wait a minute. I used to wish I was a guy. I wished it hard. But then I found out guys are best in little bits. The time it takes to walk home in the snow. The time it takes to fuck. They press themselves into you and make themselves beautiful. Sharp, aching, cutting, shooting. Pain strands me, makes me stand out. I'm all silver, burning in a chair in the middle of the room, the room too bright. The doctor gone. The doctor doesn't know. And even if he knew, what could he do?

* * *

Dear Roni —

It's your ever-hopeful sister with a word of wisdom. Are you going to start looking for a job soon? I only ask because you should be able to take care of yourself. There's really nobody else can do it for you — you know how that Christian song goes. (And don't worry, I won't say any more about Our Savior.) Anyway, I've got my own place and all, but there wouldn't be room for two here. And anyway, Ted and me are seeing more of each other, which means he's over here more.

I still think about mom a lot, do you? I have a pair of earrings of hers that would look great on you. We should get together for coffee — maybe at Mena's — and I'll give them to you.

Lots of love and luck — Paula

SPANG

I have made a gun of my own design. The concept has fascinated me throughout childhood, and now, with the high school metal shop at my disposal, I found the means to build it. It is a simple apparatus, requiring no explosive, loaded with tailor's pins, which it shoots up to 100 feet. I carry it with me at all times.

Why shoot pins? It's not about damage; it's about accuracy. I made the sight using a little vernier, which controls crosshairs. If my aim is steady, I can burst a light bulb across a room. I can shoot a bird in the back yard, or I can shoot the house cat crouched and stalking the bird. The beauty of my gun is its silence. It is not strong enough to kill, but a pin inflicts some pain. It is completely unexpected, without report or flash, causing brief panic.

I'm proud of my invention. Its principal mechanism is a spring-loaded plunger which propels the pins through a narrow copper pipe. I release the plunger with a trigger. To reset the trigger and reload, I pull back on a plastic arm. It's an actual arm, from an action figure I had when I was a kid. As the plunger is pulled against the resistance of the spring, a new pin falls into the chamber. This is the delicate part: a gravity feed regulated by two tiny ratchet gears. It was the most difficult to perfect. I spent many hours testing tiny springs, filing and resetting the metal teeth. In the end, naturally, the simplest design works best. My little gun holds up to fifty pins at ready.

I have shop three periods a week, two metal, one wood. Mr. Schark teaches metal shop. He's an arrogant asshole. Mostly he just lets us work on our projects while he sits in his office. But he's always watching. If he knew I was making a pin shooter he'd get me expelled. Metal shop feels like prison. Wood shop is different, even fun. It's taught by Mr. Fisch.

I'm good at shop because I concentrate on the details. I guess I got that from my dad. My mom disappeared when I was little, so I spend most of my time with my dad. He's a cartographer. Most maps now are based on satellite photos and computer projections, but there's still a need for the old-fashioned, skilled grunt with a pen and ink. The big publishers employ hundreds of these guys, all in one huge room under fluorescent lights, with magnifying glasses on retractable arms. Not my dad. He works freelance. A freelance cartographer. That's unusual. The small publishers, maybe they just use maps to illustrate an article or something, so they don't need a cartographer on staff.

Wait a minute. You never mentioned your mother before. You say she disappeared?

Yeah. Rosetta. That's her name. My dad calls her Rose. He and I were out one day — I was five — and when we got home she wasn't there. Didn't die, just gone. No note, nothing. It left a big hole in my dad's life. I don't remember that much about her. There's a photograph of the two of them from before I was born. She's a lot shorter than my dad. Short and skinny, tiny really, with a round face and a bush of black hair. She's doing this little twist with her back, her hand on her hip, looking up at my dad. You can't help but love her. She sings a lot, hums when she moves around the house. Not at all like my dad. He works all the time, works and worries. He worries about the true shape of things. He thinks he knows where my mom is, and if he could just get an accurate picture of the place in his mind he'd be able to go and find her. Problem is, there's always something there that he doesn't see for what he does see. That's the way a mapmaker's mind works. You have to be selective. The thing you want to see stands in front of what you really want to see. Or at least that thing, what you want to see, suggests there's something else, something better, behind it or out of reach.

I guess I got a lot of my ideas from my dad. Even my fascination with pins. A technician like my dad, a mapmaker, uses pins all the time, to hold the paper steady, to locate and hold a tiny point. But still, growing up with just one parent, a kid compensates. A kid needs to believe the world is whole, that it's what he sees. My main experience of my mom's absence has been through my dad. It never leaves him alone. He's obsessively scrupulous. But there have been times when he's lost entire blocks of function. Once I found him squatting behind a bush in the back year, taking a crap. I had to bring him inside and show him we have a toilet. He hardly every talks about my mom, but he's always preoccupied. And every couple of months it rips through the surface. The scariest instance was the time we were driving and all of a sudden he forgets how to work the car. He's just sitting there in the driver's seat, hands in his lap, going 60, looking all around, toying with the knobs on the dashboard. Luckily he took his foot off the gas, so we gradually stopped, but I had to reach over and steer us to the side of the road. I'm maybe ten, eleven at the time. But it has been over the last year or so that he has gotten really bad. He shows up at school in the middle of the day, takes me out of class. No explanation. We get on the highway and he started talking about coordinates. He has a new map which he's found in some odd place he associates with my mom, like the magazine section of the supermarket where she shops, or in an old textbook from the charity bazaar at our church. A geological map of Pennsylvania showing concentrations of bituminous, anthracite, all types of coal. A timber map of Okanagan County, Washington, with logging roads. He pores over these random maps, and he comes up with some unique way of reading them. Forget the key, he knows mapmaking inside out, and he's convinced each map hides a trace of mom. When she stopped being here, with us, she became there, waiting for us. Cartography is an art that's independent of subject matter. Maybe the coordinates on a map add up to my mom's birthday, or the colors remind him of her favorite sweater. Once he drew coordinates on a US Geologic Survey map of western West Virginia by connecting the letters of her name –R — O — S — E — T — T — A —then triangulating from those lines. Maps are completely open to interpretation.

The problem starts when we go out to these places looking for her. We drive, sometimes for days to a place in the middle of nowhere. We live in the car on bottled water and those little packages of peanut but-ter crackers. My dad won't talk about anything but his theory of interpreting the current map. I listen, and he starts to make sense. By the time we get where we're headed, I have my own ideas about where we'll find mom. These destinations are always obscure. We stop on the side of the road and proceed to hike, or climb, even swim. We carry everything with us. I designed this case out of wood I salvaged from a packing crate. I used the metal hinges, hasps and handle from an old suitcase. I keep it packed and ready at all times with everything we might need: theodolite, scroll, alidade compass, flashlight, pencils, plumb and line. A crank-up radio. I can imagine a map of radio waves. And, of course, my pin gun.

Good as my dad is a drawing and reading maps, he gets confused out in the corresponding world. He gets real quiet and upset when he can't find the spot we're looking for, let alone any sign of my mom. I take him by the hand, and lead him on. I talk to him. "That hachure there, dad, that must be that red ridge up ahead." "Your coordinate's at 32", dad, that's mom's age. We'll have to get over this gully." And since topographic maps always consider altitude, there's a lot of digging involved. That's a problem when things are so uncertain. The world is all irregularities. We diminish our objective, reduce our expectations, but at the same time the search becomes more urgent and desperate. We're not actually looking for my mom any more, but for some clue. A piece of her jewelry, someone we could ask, a tree or a sign on the ground. And when nothing makes sense out there, we start to dig. I do most of the shovel work. I get signals from my dad. He's increasingly remote, scouting terrain. He points to a spot, and I know he wants me to dig. Connect the dots. Four paces northwest, seven paces south, three feet down. No dig is ever completely empty. It's all in how you read it. Patience, perseverance, attention to detail. I'm digging—this one's got to be four feet deep—and when I look up I can't see my dad. Then I notice two tiny figures silhouetted way over on the top of that far ridge. I watch them for a second. They seem to embrace, then they are gone. I go back to digging.

So that's what brought you here, to Tombigbee. But where's your father?

Gone on ahead. Tombigbee's the map he left me. It's very large and precise, down to the varieties of pine creeping up the hillside. The fewer people there are in your life, the fewer maps you need. That spring, it's just an ink dot, that's what I'm after, but it keeps moving. Must've migrated twenty feet west since this was drawn. Of course, it's an old map. Any map's like a snapshot, stop action, so any trace I might find of my mom is probably off true by now. But my dad drew an "R" right there by that dot.

Digging around, I'm finding rose colored shale. This is how I get information about her. I never really knew her, so I dig. The soil is loose, not too rocky, just little stones. Cowries. Did she have a necklace of cowries? Over there I went down almost six feet before I hit water. Pine needles, loam and lots of crawly things. Remnants of bone near the surface about eight feet from the spring. I'm careful to uncover and lift each piece. If I don't concentrate on what I'm doing, flesh grows at the joints and spreads. Then hair. Is it human hair? My mom's hair's bright, dark brown. When I concentrate, the hair falls off, the flesh decays. That's hard work. My mind wants to run to its conclusion. The digging wears me out and occupies me, but this time I start to cry. My legs are weak. I sit down. My hands feel stubby, my fingers hard to bend. Cork. My teeth don't feel right in my mouth. I notice I have a cut, a pimple, a bruise, a rash. I'm scared. The map's no help. The closer you look, the less it reveals.

So this is where you end up, here, now.

Lost.

You need direction, so. You won't find that here, or anywhere, for that matter. This world is a veil of unattainable desires. Direction has to come from within. Consider Our Lord Jesus Christ. He too spent His life searching, nor was he of this earth. He was as a breath of smoke carried on a breeze. He came and went, came and went, and those few who knew him were in awe. He had no map. He left no footprint where he walked. His very flesh did not define him, and yet like any animal His nostrils flared at the scent of meat. Did I say that He was not a man? Nay, He was more man than any man. He hungered and He lusted, and He acted, yes, He acted on his bodily urges. His anger through the valley rolled as thunder. You could in no way fathom the depth of His anguish. To be a man and yet to be denied mortality! What man is this? Can He from His Mistress, Father, Son, the Nether Presence plead forgiveness? He is debased. He is slain. Only to revive and to be slain again. As the affairs of His Kingdom cloud and darken He can but endure. Daily, hourly, murdered in the trenches. Gassed, shot, bombed, or worse, denied sustenance, wounds festering without treatment, thoroughly neglected. How are we to comprehend His defilement? Limb by gland our sensate selves decay. If blame there be —and yes, faith is a friable support — where place the blame for this corruption? Look not to your maps, young man, for no device made by man can transcend its maker, whose existence obfuscates the Kingdom of a Vengeful God. Look not to the body, with its crude betrayals, and looks not to the mind, which is as a caged and frenzied vermin. Look to Jesus only, son. To him, whom you will never see, nor hear, nor taste, your bitter flame surrender.

NEIGHBORHOOD

You sit down in your chair. You settle yourself. You pick up your book or your magazine, and this is what you read:

I was one of the ones who killed that guy. That's what you want to hear, right? There were three of us, me, Little Richie, and Jimmy Blunt. We tracked the guy for half the night, then we did him. But killing isn't enough for you, is it? Killing isn't any-thing extraordinary these days. You want irony. You want to believe in the killing. A good story, some entertainment, something to keep your mind occupied. Well, I haven't got that. There's a lot of killing going on around here. Each killing calls forth another killing. There's no particular reason. Put down your magazine and think about it. You know it's true. I'd have to try hard to make you think I'm some kind of monster. That's what you expect. Well, I don't care about your expectations. You and me, we're very much alike. We're in this for the same reason.

Here. Hold my glass for a second. I've got to take a whiz.

Now, Little Richie, he should have cashed in years ago, after that accident he had. That left him all crippled up. He didn't quit, but he could have, you know? You can see it on his face. He keeps going, but he doesn't know why. He's in pain, but he keeps pushing. It's like the reason is just in front of him, right there in the air, and he's pushing himself for-ward to get it. The reason for what? I don't know. Neither does he.

I guess we're all loners in this neighborhood. Cipoletti the fitter. Grundy the corpse. Pope the cop, Palacci the lathe, Opielski the stamp. Furman the loom… Is this interesting to you? Well, it's not there anymore. Most every one dead. Dead or just gone. I pass people on the street I know I know, but I don't recognize them. The stores, the potted plants, the signs, the little things that make a neighborhood, all gone. The streets and buildings are still there, but they make these noises, day and night. You walk past a house and it calls out your name, or it laughs at you.

It's a lot of work, keeping a body up, pulling the thing through life. I could give you a description, but I don't want to make it that easy for you.

The neighborhood is my livelihood, it's my life. When I go out into it, which I do most every night, I never come back. I've been warned. I go walking with a stranger who holds a power over the movement of traffic, the denizens, the swing of my arms and my heartbeat. I'm lost. What's around that next corner? The opportunity to rest. I lay my troubles on the curb. Before I know it, I've fallen asleep, and it's the next night, or the next.

A terrible fear comes up in me.

Jimmie Blunt is a good man to talk to. Very down to earth. Always got a plan. Jimmie used to work the ovens. He's seen it all. "A scar is not the same as the wound that made it," he'll say. Jimmie knows how to make a guy feel secure. I'm down, y'know, I'm troubled, and Jimmie finds me. Without a word he's got his arm underneath my arm. He reaches around my torso, coming close, and my senses are filled with the scent of fresh-cut lumber. Jimmie Blunt.

I remember when I met Jimmie, when he was a dog. There's always dogs loose in the neighborhood. Nobody feeds them or pays them much mind, but when they gang up they can cause a person trouble. Even one by hisself. That's what happened with me and Jimmie. I'm out this one evening at the corner of Fifth and Brown, I think it was, or maybe Seventh. Anyway, I'm on my back, admiring the streetlights, and I hear this growl. Now I've learned to keep my distance from these wild dogs, but in this case, I didn't have much choice, being on the ground already, so I just ignored him. But the dog was sniffing around my feet, and when I moved my hand to try and shoo him off, he growled again. I couldn't ignore him any more, so I propped myself up on my elbows and just stared at him, mean as can be, figuring to show him who's boss. Well, he commenced to growling even louder, and showing his teeth, with the fur standing up on his back. I knew I'd have to take action, as I fixed that dog's eyes with mine and I says, firm as can be, "Reveal thyself, common cur. Thy name, Impostor in the fur." With this, the dog whimpers. He tries to back off, then he begins to twitch. He falls on the ground and right before my eyes he turns into a human man. All I can say is "Huh?" I don't move. Then this guy says to me, "Don't you know me? I'm Jimmie Blunt." But I never saw him before.

You should back off. You're standing a little close. That's better. Now I'm going to tell you about the killing.

Three. In the aggregate they wouldn't even fill a man's palm. Each singly, with it's shiny black facets and unique refractive qualities, distinct. Yellow for

the oak and maple which once populated this valley, cleared for agriculture, in turn supplanted by brick and industry. Purple for the herd, the minds of men, stampede and the failure of resolution. All the colors. Coal.

I hold mine tight against the night wind, coming up from a dreamless sleep. I'm no longer young. This hurts, that hurts. I'm a little dizzy. It takes a few tries for me to get on my feet. I'm up. I go off to find the other two.

It's a dark and stormy night. I can say that with total confidence.

I find Jimmie Blunt by the corner of what used to be Fifth and Dauphin, only not it's Eighth and Somerset. He's sitting on a stoop talking to the bottle of Bull 40 he's got in a bag. The coal is on the step beside him. He's drooling a little. Now I know Jimmie to be a little jumpy and quick to strike if you sneak up on him, so I walk out into the middle of the street and come up on him slow, in full view.

"Hey Jimmie. S'up?"

Jimmie doesn't look at me or move. "Fuck you," he says.

I sit down beside him.

The moon moves over and down, from over St Bruno's to just at the top of the row of houses on Cambria.

We don't have to look for Little Richie; he finds us. He doesn't get along that well with Jimmie, so he comes up on my side. I can tell he's got something on his mind. He's walking fast, a little crooked, almost like he's swimming, that ugly face first, pushing the air away in from of him. He's holding that lump of coal in his fist. Shifting from foot to foot, anxious. He doesn't wait for anybody to say hello.

"He swallowed all three — we was gone, free — all around us — gold! — where's that coal? — here it is — beat 'im up bad — a good heist — birds, I tell ya — big black ones — I'd a killed 'im — right off the guy's finger — he gives me coal — here it is —gone — I chased him but he — more than a hundred of 'em — birds — everyplace, flapping, flying off — swallowed — the rings."

Richie leads the way.
It isn't hard to find the guy. Jimmie Blunt's a little groggy, and he leans on me as we walk, but he comes around after awhile. Richie takes us to Third and Norris, right by the park, which he won't walk through because that's where him and this other guy — the guy we're looking for — made the hit. Instead we head up Third to Cambria, then over to Fifth. Down Fifth half a block, then through the alley that runs behind the houses these to Sixth, which we traverse, passing diagonally across the fallow lot where once my father labored in Steuben's Confectionery, long before the bottom fell out of the candy market and the place suspiciously burned. Need I describe more of our trajectory? Suffice it to say we adhered to a direction approximating 29 degrees northwest of the path of the moon — brilliantly gibbous until we located the first, and then the entire flock of corvus corax. But here we are at Ninth and Wyomissing. This is where you get off. I know you type. You're only interested in the bloody parts. Well, there was plen-ty of blood when we found that guy. We had to cut open his stomach to get what we wanted. You need proof? Here, look. I'm wearing one of those rings. But you'll have to use your imagination for the rest. I've got better things to do than entertain you.

THE CITY

Let me describe the city—this large sector of the city—as a map, or an endless three-dimensional model seen from above. It is an old city, built quick-ly and then abandoned. Move over it slowly, as if in flight, but don't descend. That would be a mistake. It is too dark, its streets and blocks too regular. They go on indefinitely, without destination. Not only are all the lights, which once lit the street-corners and storefronts, extinguished, but the scene itself seems to absorb and erase what light might come its way. Nobody. Many of the buildings seem truncated, gray and mute to their history. Many are sealed with cinderblock, and where there is a win-dow, it is a thorough, unreflecting black.

You will have to imagine who I am. After all, how could I describe myself? Like anyone else, I'm fascinated by my image in a mirror, but that is only a glimpse, something fleeting, which immediately turns into a question. I can't even retrieve the question. Ask me. Ask me anything. I'd welcome the dis-traction.

I could really use a rest. I've been running like this for several blocks, and each time I think I'm near the end, it proves not to be the end at all. Only another boarded window or a gated entry. The end keeps leaping ahead.

If you would fall in with me, keep the pace, I'm sure
That I could shake this fear. Here is an emblem. A ribbon and seal that make my letter authentic. Yes, it is stained and the ink has run. We've been out in the rain. But nonetheless…

What is written beneath this seal is more true than this dark street. Please keep up with me. No, I did-n't write it, and when I read it I always get it wrong. It is more myself than mine. It is more yourself than you imagine.

It grants us passage. Like all stories, it doesn't know where to begin. It touches down here and there, a confession hidden behind a bush, a crime. The author was watch-ing his own flesh dry, distend and slough off. That's when he wrote this note.

What is a scar? Site of some pleasure. When you wake, from the dream, to the room, it is the room first, as if it were the extent of your body, confine of all sensa-tion. A wall is a complex amalgam. An idea. Break it apart and such out the seeds. Break plaster, lath, the violent, open secret. Build a city to dispute it. Please run a little faster. There's something in the story catching up with us.

What are you afraid of? Some stray vocable won't dissolve, follows us like a bat. Worse, its erratic is its plan regardless. You are its accident. It was you invited the unwanted spell into the house in the first place. Are you sleeping? The author leans over your unguarded ear and whispers the sequence of sounds. They are poorly-born. They thrash about sullying the air around you, and you take them in in thin, resisting threads.

Sinew and neglect, a vision to accommodate capital. Locked to a brick lot their children look alike, an absence in the speech which resonates toward labor. Take away work its pain remains, to be inflicted. Keep moving. Shadows sliding on concrete want to take the story away. I can stay a step or two ahead. Can you?

Cough. Eighteen killed this very corner. Troops on horseback, cars, the children organized gangs and lived in cracks to live at all. The women died, watching it. Poison spray, a wave of helicopter raids.

The city is so full of its dead that it has no room. It is empty and stretches out to take up any thought of escape. Impose the city on the plain. It is a phantom, but it is all you can imagine. You cannot imagine the life of the plain without oracle, solvent, lush infestation. The closer you look, the less you perceive. One street going forward, brittle and breaking apart, oblivious.

Let's go. Every splinter in the shower of splinters has a memory. We have our own requirements. Those murders are in the past, and so are we. Keep up. I won't put up with you holding me back. I don't know you and I don't like you.

It's time for me to get rid of you. Does that sound coarse? I've got my own survival to think of. Here is a ditch running beside the street. I know, you see them everywhere, full of garbage and scummy water. This one is nothing special. Once, perhaps only once, an adolescent girl could be observed in one of these ditches. She would be lying there, her face turned to the side and her ass higher than her head, kicking her feet like a dog hit by a car. You see, I remember things. My frame of reference is much broader than yours. You are just a visitor here.You try to take it all in,read the decay. But the past has no reality. Wood, brick, mortar and glass.

They rot when you look at them. I have made a meeting place of substance. It is porous. To look at it is to enter, by degree. It is cavernous, with rough walls dripping fire. Why have you come? Who have you come to meet? Here are two columns of people, one to the left and one to the right, regularly spaced. A gauntlet. Avert your eyes. They don't see you. Everyone has his own problems and hopes. You could be out of here in the blink of an eye if you'd move a little faster. Keep walking. Every step your feel sink deeper into the ground.

MY COMPANION

I suppose I would have started out regardless, had I not been coerced, but now, circumstances in their ineluctable sway accumulating, I will never know my own will. One foot falls before the other, or one succeeds, or perhaps one is betrayed by its mirror twin, it's hard to say, but I find my gait irregular, foreign. I am a kernel in a dark husk, a sound of rushing air continually in my ears. Why must it be, this confusion of tense, events which led me up to this point, if, indeed, a point it be, brick upon brick or oar stroke after stroke, have it however you like, will not stand of follow, statins no logic? None of the moment, anyway, which moves away.

Indecision, uncertainty, arbitrary choice, a man shifts back and forth. Each thing man made, each natural phenomenon, whatever stands out from the rest in the impetuous perceptual flow first bursts, then near dies out, then stutters into memory to signify. The sign, I'll say, posting a note to myself for future contemplation, is more a function of need than of transcendence.

Such is the admix reflex and anxious agitation, I cannot rightly sequence, motor or potential, whether a voice alone can power this cartoon one frame to the next, when that voice issues, to wit: "Mind your stirrups, Sir." Indeed, for an ambulator odd, I've maintained a dorsal posture, anus fore-most, both legs powerlessly akimbo, waving east and west like an infant, a dreaming remnant of the sylvan gully in which I so recently lay.

"I'd the impression I was afoot. Beg pardon."

"Ah! So you are! My mistake," as if such civil repartee permitted any nocturnal maggot intimacy, to match host step for step, to mingle exhalations, his flesh far too close to mine. My interlocutor stands, or I should say strides, with difficulty keeping up, the question of beginning moot, we're moving now, roughly to my navel, uninvited. Were it not for certain secondary characteristics, most notably a pro-fusion of keratinous growth at every visible, and no doubt those hidden from the polite eye as well, orifice, I could not guess his gender. The voice is high and thin, the scent of roasting chestnut, shoulders and buttocks rolling, I'd nearly feel a stirring down below were it not for my repulsion. So the sexual predicament flees, propelled, or so it seems, on a flume from a nozzle virtually obstructed. Its residue remains, a gauze of vague fears gradually fulminating about this hining stump, my companion, so recently a mere intruder.

It could be advised, before we take another step, or leastwise amid step, each determining all to follow, to attempt a calculation of eventualities. Unaccustomed to the plural narrative, I cannot. Were person first and singular, my fair territory, I'd postulate an endgame. I could resurrect, were any past more than fiction, the ease with which I, adolescent, desired peach, damp contact, the fatuous mechanics luring every man, with all physical and mental faculties at the beck of such concupiscence, unquestionably. Note, however, the conditional voice throughout this suffering paragraph, part light part shadow, partly born. This voice, though interior, speaks volumes I prefer to hide.

But society is it sown calamity, however familiar, and even in advance of articulation I've named my timeless companion melancholy. Fear and loathing in the incipient coupling, yes, impending violence. Should I choose to speed it up, he falters; should I indicate a gee, he gruffly mumbles and chews on his haw. I strike out with my elbows, contumacious at the bridle, knees sharp, a quick feint, if narrative at all, utterly conspicuous, while he obtusely whittles. Have we agreed upon a beginning? Why dwell on it? Here's the specter of intercourse and destination.

My companion, the snake: "Are you prepared?"

I, near out of breath: "I note however cramped the grammar of thought, speech barely spits." I can only hope this figure will satisfy him, for I have neither the comprehension nor the stamina to go on. My wrists with thinnest straps of rime feel bound, my identity confused. I feel the cockroach crawling on my thigh, and dull aversion spiraling wide.

The cockroach: "You cannot say where you are going, nor hazard the course that brought you here, here, too, a mere sensory smear. You deliver yourself to random consequence, stray bullet, venereal sepsis."

Have I not already said as much? Were it not for my companion's threatening tone this exchange might lapse into muffled dope and comedy. Yet he with his arachnidian eye fixes me, and I am again undone. My defense falters: "And you have something better?"

The bud of our succeeding questions on my lips I swoon imagining any answer palpable, mine and it compressed. Oh brief respite, would he answer! The bone of his shoulder tight beneath my chin and throat, hip to socket pressed, to reach around as to my only pubis, unashamed at how the spider's legs move rhythmically to my stroke. The moment passes, it could be said, like smoke. I am hung up and abated, alone.

The spider does not speak. From out my throat and taut to some distant and obscure objective gut holds me to an arc, the one pole helpless love, no other word for it, for the prod of my examiner, the other, dread. I stumble forth and back, capitulating any aggression which to the sum of my esteem con-tributes. I am humbled, contrite, as blinded feeling in the brush and crud about me fro my little friend, with him terrified, without him not. That I have fall-en to my fours should bring us nearer, if only corporeally, a juxtaposition I so recently abhorred, and now crave, if only to again abjure. Furthermore, his question recedes, no doubt betraying the paucity of my attention. There is neither profit nor redemption in the promise to amend and honor; it is near and it is gone at once, a bat awing.

Nor can I fix a terminus, any future elusive. Here and then diminished, I must retrieve a correspondence. From my quadruped I fall to postures increasingly feral, reversing genesis, as it were, the closer to what is called vaingloriously earth but is in practice mud to be, all dignity sham, however dimly ascertained. Weasel, mouse, millipede, then forsaking limbs entirely, slug, worm, slimy thing. The anomaly expands in ratio to my degradation. What is it?

PINWHEEL

I am tired, having walked such a long way uphill, but even my fatigue is light, like a white jacket which comes easily off and falls behind me. Over that wooded rise a rising medallion, jeweled song of every color, and at each door a girl. Some are red, some blue, some yellow—iron, steel and brass. If I move toward any one of them she is naked, bowing at the waist and inviting me in. I choose instead to lie back here on the grass as the pinwheel spins over me. Reach into the picture and pull it close. Feel my strength. Even as I pull the little girls from their hiding places, even as I crush them against my chest, there are more, offering themselves. They are squealing, each squeal a red smear on a perfect blue sky. So beautiful. Everyone is watching. They cheer as I squeeze the spinning thing, and squeeze it squirting up like a tornado, the girls' sounding like a moan inside. Then going black.

I come down in the back of Luddy's car, flat on my back with the silhouettes of oak branches flipping by down upside against a deep deep sky. It seems cooler, darker, so we must be getting close to Temper's place up in the hills. I'm a little stiff, hurt in my right should and ribs. Can't say how long I was out. Jane and Luddy up front look straight ahead saying nothing.

I groan a little to let them know I'm awake. Jane makes a little sideways look at Luddy; Luddy grips the wheel tighter and adjusts himself in his seat. I see his jaw muscle move. Nothing more. Strange how nobody's talking, especially Jane. She was my old lady before Luddy, and we're still good friends. Luddy goes 60,65, even on these winding old roads, up and up.

I sit back, try to remember the dream, play it over. I like that. Mostly I remember the colors, yellow, gold, and red, like polished brass spinning disks you could walk into. Smooth and ripe as cantaloupe, but metal, a liquid metal singing in my arms and thighs. Funny how on PCP such a good feeling is really the same as a terrible feeling, the ache all over fear like the car might drive right into the side of the hill right, into the rock and underground. Like Jane and Luddy might want to do me in.

Finally we get to Temper's place; I know it 'cause of the sound of gravel under the wheels. I pull myself up between the two front seats and notice Jane's hand wrapped in a towel. She sees me looking at it so we don't say anything about it. We pull up to the cabin and Jane gets right out and walks, a little stiff, it seems, but quick, holding that hand, straight up to the cabin. Luddy kind of waits around.

I'm still kind of dazed, things coming back to me slow. That hurt in my side must be worse than I though since I have to catch my breath once just getting out of the back seat, then a sharp pain standing up. I hold on to the side of the car, with Luddy there just pretending not to see me. I count four other cars there in the driveway, none I recognize, and nobody around. Must all be inside. Didn't know Temper was having a party.

I feel Luddy's eyes on me all the way across the drive and up the front porch steps. Door's open.

Mostly people just standing and sitting around there in the smoke, some talking, but most stop when I walk in. Big guys, mostly, some I recognize, like Temper, Al, Mankie, most I don't, all looking at me. A radio all by itself in another room. It's dark in the room, and it takes a few seconds for my eyes to adjust. I probably look like I'm staring, but for a second I think I see something black and squirming in a big bowl they're got there on the floor in the middle of the room. One guy's holding a knife. Then I notice Mankie looking at my hand, and I stare him back, put it behind me, I don't know why. Never liked Mankie. It all makes me uncomfortable, so I just kind of nod and walk into the hallway toward the kitchen. On the way I look at my hand. It's got blood on it, a real smear, on the sleeve, too, real ugly, and it's not mine.

I know Temper's got another room to this place, a big room he keeps a lot of stuff in, and it's got a sink and toilet. Door's off this hallway, just before the kitchen. I can hear Jane's voice, all freaked, and some other woman talking, from the kitchen as I turn the knob and push in.

Room's empty, smells rank, like nothing's moved in here for years. Boxes and what look like cages along the far wall, a stuffed armchair, paneling coming off the near, no lights. The sink as I remember it's beside the one window, which is propped up with a stick and looks out over the driveway. I can feel that pain running down my right side again as I walk toward it.

First thing I notice looking in the mirror over the sink is a big cut on my head over my eye. Look at the thing's enough to make me feel sick, and I lean and grab the sink. Funny I hadn't felt it before. No washcloth here, so I run water into my hands and splash it on my forehead. The cold water feels good, so I do my whole face and neck, then get to work scrubbing the blood off my hand. Won't come out of my sleeve, so I just roll it up. Breeze coming in the window feels good on the cold water. Things are getting a little clearer. I think back to Jane, how she wouldn't look or talk to me.

For a moment, things are pretty peaceful. I'm still at the sink, but looking out the window, past the cars out front to the dust on the leaves of the trees, hearing the little brickle sound from the creek runs beside Temper's. Another fragment of the dream comes back, a smiling girl floating toward me from a shady spot on the side of a hill. Maybe my head's still buzzed, since I'm watching the sunbeams that way and don't hear my name the first time some-body calls it.

"Pete."

It's Jane's voice. "Pete."

I don't even turn to say it to the door, but keep looking out the window. "In here." I hear the handle turn, the door open. Jane's behind me.

"Pete, you've got to get out of here."

"Why. What's going on?"

"You really don't know, do you?"

I don't answer . I'm still looking out the window, at Luddy's car now, seeing the trunk is up and some-body, probably Luddy, bent over pulling on some-thing heavy in there.

"These people don't want you here, Pete."

"What people? You mean Temper? Let him tell me himself. And who are these other people?

"That's not what matters. They think you'll bring trouble."

Outside, Luddy's still pulling something out of the trunk, when suddenly I can see part of what it is. Just the tip, the foot end of a sleeping bag over the lip of the trunk, and Luddy leans back in a continues tugging. It's my sleeping bag. I've never seen another one that's bright yellow like mine.

Jane must've seen Luddy, too, and her voice becomes urgent. "Pete, you've got to get away from here! Now!"

I can feel the hair on my neck standing up. I hear the screen door slam and Temper comes striding down to Luddy's car and pulls Luddy up by the shoulder. Whatever he says I can't make out. They're both yelling at once. Whatever it is, Temper's not buying it, and it looks like he's about to smack Luddy.

Then from behind me, Jane again, "...you've got to..."

I turn around and face her. Her face is all contorted, scared shitless. "Fuck you, Jane! What the fuck are you trying to do! That thing in the car, that's not mine!"

Her face is red, her eyes puffy with tears. Her mouth is all trembly. She can't answer, only nod. I shouldn't do it, but I suddenly hate the bitch. I swing, hard, and catch her beside the eye.

When she goes down, Jane makes a little scream, loud enough somebody must have heard it in the hallway. Those people will know what happened. Can't go out that way.

I turn back to the window and start climbing out. My side and my arm have gotten stiffer, and the pain sharper, and my landing, real awkward after falling about six feet from the window, hard as hell. The cabin is up on blocks, so I roll under into the shadow to figure my next move. Lying there, my whole arm is throbbing and it's hard to breathe. Lots of running, and the screen door slamming. My dream. The girl reaches me. She's all vapor, like blue powder, but warm, covering my body. Her eyes are yellow, and fused with mine as she wraps herself around me. She holds me. It's like a little cartoon when I see Temper come out from behind Luddy's car. He's breathing hard, and from under the cabin I can't see Luddy. Temper shouts something toward the porch, the people on the porch, and then he looks. He looks straight at me.

(untitled)

Alan's mother is out there somewhere. At least that's what we say about the recently dead, isn't it? On the other side of this glass it's raining, early winter night, just plain nasty. And she's out there, out of her body, stretching out and moving among the parked cars, the rocks and litter, the trees at the edge of the parking lot, the multitude of makeshift crypts, looking for someplace, even temporary, to rest until the wind or an ignorant kick from some kid dislodges her and she has to move her tatters on.

It feels funny, sitting here in the car tonight, wait-ing for him. I mean, I've done it many times when Alan's been travelling, but I've never had news like this to give him. The car usually feels big and friendly, powerful and full of life. It gets me what I want and I take for granted. Now I see what it really is. I'm here alone in a cold, metal capsule, darker even than outside, with raindrops on the glass inches from my face.

Not that I'll miss Alan's mom. Seems she never left me alone. Even now I feel what I always felt when I saw her. This weird insinuation in my body. First a tingling sensation in my lower spine, then a little sweat in the crack of my butt. "Alan," she'd say, "your grandmother raised me to be a lady, but your father wouldn't let me stay at home." What the fuck was she after? "Alan," I'd say, "do you think she wants us to have kids? Does she want me to get a job?" And he'd just shake his head. He never had the goddamned spine to challenge her. It's just as well she went with a heart attack, quick.

Thinking about her brings back the sensation in my ovaries, or what I've come to think is a lack of sensation. I mean, I'm not usually aware of my ovaries. Just sometimes, like now, I feel an emptiness that's really troubling. It's like a loose belt, like a gap in my belly.

I guess what really bothered me about Alan's mom wasn't so much what she said as what she didn't need to say, and didn't even know could be said. After all, she pretty much acted out the same script over and over. But put Alan in front of her and he'd be her mirror, nodding and repeating platitudes on cue, disagreeing only when disagreement was safe. There was never room for me in any of that.

I can be a mirror, too. We may be afraid of them, but the dead aren't aliens. I've been sitting still in this cold car for fifteen minutes, so maybe my body feels stiff and numb. But it's not possessed. The face on the inside of the window is my own, reflected. I can make it large. It sprouts orange hair, a monkey face in its black halo. Bare my teeth it's a lion's face. I can beat back the numbness. Breathe again.

I feel that fist of wind against the car. To me, it's a very specific sensation. But dead folks, all the dead, anything that's lived and hasn't yet rested, are that wind. They move it with all the anxiety of their knowing. What meaning can they find in powerlessness and continual movement? They have no choice.

I'll tell him in a few minutes. I know how I'll do it. I'll wait until he's in the car and settled. I'll start the engine, get the heater running, but I won't pull out. He'll look at me, sort of aware that the routine is a little different. Then I'll say, "Alan, I have bad news. Your mother had a heart attack today. She's gone." I'll watch his face.

Here comes his train at last. It's so huge, the whole place rumbles with it. The wind stops. I've got to get ready, clear my head. Breathe. Everything will be different between Alan and me after this. What will be different?

I chose Alan, I know, but I can't say I ever really "fell in love" with him. So maybe it's me I don't fully trust. But nothing he says every reveals who he really is or what he feels. What is the tenderness between us? Uncertainty. Not my uncertainty or his uncertainty, but the mutual. The unacknowledged inflection, the uncustomary gesture that can't be repeated. These are physical things. You can't know what they mean.

There's the conductor, the passengers coming down the stairs. There's Alan. He looks so tall, young and unruffled, darker than I remember. He sees the car, and now he's running this way, holding his newspaper over his head. The bastard.

THE HAWK

He said to call him Rodney, a name I don't for a moment believe. But what else could I do? That was the name he gave me, so I call him Rodney. "Hey, Rodney!" He doesn't look back. He must have heard me, but he's pretty far ahead now, picking his way down over the rocks in the dark.

"Hey, Rodney!" That must not be his name. That's why he doesn't answer me. But what choice have I got now? I've got to follow him. I can't see the path — if there is one — only rocks and shrubbery. It was his idea to walk down to the ocean. I was perfectly happy back at the hawk, talking, just the two of us under the new moon in the parking lot. But once he had the idea, he was gone, looking for a path in the bushes, over the edge.

The way he moves. Like a wrestler, kind of bulky, but getting there, and not without grace. I can just make him out. Everything I can do to follow his lead, step up this high rock, hold on to this branch to swing my weight down, the way Rodney did, onto the next series of low ones. I can see his tee shirt bobbing back and forth, though not his arms. Too dark. But I can follow the broad white triangle of his back, imagine its muscles, its sharp reach, release, support, flex and stretch.

The beach is further off than it seemed. To our left, as we descend obliquely, it complains, occasionally breaking its own monotony with an unexpected crash. There is a little wind, I think, and my own arrhythmic breathing. The bushes crowd around me, scratching my arms and pulling at my clothing. They are larger than any man, obscuring the sky. The lights from the bar are gone behind me, up behind the embankment.

I try to keep my eyes on Rodney. He seems to float away from me, visible on a straight stretch of the path, then disappearing. In and out of view. When I am unable to see him, I focus on what is already a memory: the angular bulk of his thighs, pressing on his shorts, his legs slightly spread as if ready to carry him away from me, which, in fact, they did, leaving memory there under the bugswarming light beside the bar. How can you say when you actually begin to know someone? I'd met Rodney just half an hour earlier, but his impulse to get his feet wet, to go when and where he wanted to go, was irresistible. When he'd gone, that place was hollow again, the shapes in the night again threatening. I followed.

Shit. Not I think I've lost him. I've never been good at this, this meeting, share a laugh and get acquainted. Alan, my first, used to ride me. "You're all primp and no performance." How could he not know that would hurt me all the way to here?

"You're afraid of your own sex." It's as if Alan were here in this thicket. I only hope I haven't lost the path. Keep the ocean on my left, step, careful, maybe Rodney will wait for me.

"Over this way!" the voice is to my right, up the embankment. I hesitate; the ocean seems the other way. I'm not afraid, I'd tell Alan, just getting older. "Rodney!" "Old is one word for it." No answer. Who called out to me? Up the hill a little to my right is a dark copse, a gesture, origin of the call. "You just don't know what you want. "Rodney knows the way here, not me. "…to relive forever some childhood indecision, some frailty. "Why won't he answer me? The landscape's grades of black and green, its elemental movement and its confidence, asks the question.

I know at once the voice was Rodney's, and that it is my invention. He is so self-possessed. It surely wasn't his voice, calling me off the path to surprise me with a hug. Yet it is sensible to follow this voice precisely because it is something my mind made up. I've got to provide for my own departures. I left Alan as I am leaving Rodney, left him to his own pursuits, his pride, holding my own. From this point, where I go, I go on my own. Let them follow me.

Coming up on it in the dark, the figure of my copse, my grove, alters. It was a man reclining on an elbow, then, closer, two men, one reclining, the second attending. The way there is rough. I fall, grab hold of branches, am pulled by every weed and thorn. Now directly on it, my little copse has grown. It rears before me like a black stallion. There at its base: a low opening. I'll have to crawl.

The ground is damp here under the leaves. They catch the fine mist off the ocean, collect it and drip it down, sustaining themselves. These bushes have been here for centuries, advancing slowly up a crevice of the hillside, and here, in their interior, undisturbed.

I am not here to disturb them. I advance cautiously, on all fours at first, then find the earth penetrable, my limbs entering the soil as I move forward. This interior is thick with stems and branches, yet I encounter no resistance. I push through, the stems pressing into and through my flesh. I sink. My mouth fills with the wet loam. My hair, my eye sockets, anus, spine, fill move forward, and rest.

Above me, the new moon shows a sheer crescent. There is a slight wind, which leads the leaves of the copse in a light clatter. Where it had seemed a little cold, the effects of the cold have passed; where there had been weight, weight is undifferentiated. There is no point in reflecting. Rodney did not know the way, and in losing me is lost. Each thought of him rises and is erased. My first memory of him is last. He may not have known I saw him; it hardly matters. I'd gone into the men's room at the bar to piss, and saw him in the mirror when I was standing at the urinal. He was standing up in a stall, his back to the door, which was ajar, his right arm extended to the wall to balance himself. His shorts were down, and his left hand was wrapped tightly around his penis. He rocked back and forth slowly, tightening and relaxing his grip, blood apparent in his neck.

ASCENSION

I don't usually venture into the woods anymore, at least not at night. Maybe I'm becoming a homebody in my old age. I'm content to patrol the periphery of the yard where it meets the poke and the chokecherry, with my yellow dog Baxter. One time around, before bedtime, for security.

But this time the darkest part of the woods opens up like a maw, and Baxter breaks from me and runs right in. I have to follow. Now, Baxter knows these woods by smell, but it's so dark I have to go by memory, and I'm surprised how little I remember. I stumble. Baxter is a yellow flicker, like a candle flame. These woods are full of cramps, but they don't seem to bother him. Unfamiliar things brush against my legs. I hear my heart in my head.

That's when the cramp hits me. Calf of my left leg. I go down immediately. I grab the thing. He's a good sized one, big as a rat, and he's got his whole wide jaw and both claws wrapped around my leg. The pain takes over. I start to squeeze his furry little body and he lets out this gravelly sound, like a fire blown ahead of a strong wind through brush. That sound goes on and on.

The pain continues, and the impression of that greasy fur and the small, pliant bones of the rodent stays on my hand, but as I open my eyes the wood is gone. My husband is kneeling on the floor beside the bed, shaking me, but his attention is not on me, it's beyond me, on the bedroom door. Karl's been blind going on ten years now. You'd think we would talk more, but instead we've found other ways to communicate, and we hardly talk at all. Right now, Karl looks afraid. There's nothing like the look of fear on a blind man's face. The sound I was just hearing, that rushing sound, is coming through the door.

If there's something wrong in the house, why hasn't Baxter told us?

I've wrapped my terry robe around me and I'm heading toward this dim yellow light, a light like I've never seen before, coming from the hallway. Maybe it's because I'm still a little asleep, but as I go my legs feel bandy and there's a feeling of glee in my belly, like when an airplane takes off. Each step I take seems to lift me higher.

The scriptures say that Christ was drawn to the light. The light flooded the gallery and he was absorbed, and he rose. The apostles witnessed it.

In the hallway, I can see the light coming around the kitchen door on the landing. Pushing the door open, the sound I've been hearing swells into a soft, crackling roar. Light fills the room. It is the light of fire, but it gives off no heat. It has no source and nothing is consumed.

Transubstantiation is a subject I've given some thought. What is it, at any particular moment, that holds the molecules and atoms of the familiar world together? What about you and me? A religious per-son would say the soul, at least when you're talking about people. But then you hear about the souls of animals, of trees, of all kinds of things animate and inanimate. You need to draw the line somewhere.

From my vantage up on the landing I can see very corner of the fiery room. The cramp in my left calf is still there, forcing my toe to point against my will. But in a way, the pain focuses my attention.

My first though is Baxter, who is not on the rug that's been his bed since he was a puppy. No sign of Baxter. Then I notice a few things have been moved, or changed. A glass of thick liquid has been spilled on the counter. A knife on the cutting board has left an odd stain. I don't recognize that knife. I almost see the door to the back yard closing. Then I notice the kitchen table has been moved, rotated ninety degrees and pushed against the wall. There's an envelope on the table, containing a letter, which reads:

> Berthe:
>
> Did you think the Poet was dead? Doubt, and
> my time is up. But I make time I am fastidious. I
> travel all the earth, and with absolute
> care make my selections. There is no rest
> even in death. If everything is available for
> use, then you will not find your congruence.
> Your search will be futile. I use a sharp stick
> and a stabbing motion. Fire is an indeterminate

My eyes are distracted from the paper by the sight of Baxter's face in the window over the sink. Doesn't it seem odd to me that he is there, some six feet up from the ground outside? Like I say, it's just his face, and it's almost like it's a movie of his face, the way it's floating there ringed around in the darkness by a yellow light. He's got his eyes on me and I feel a great relief. I walk toward him, into the fire.

THE PIGEON

She keeps her hands in her lap just below the edge of the desk, according to some constraint adopted when the habit was newer, but now forgotten, as the nervousness at the bottom of it all takes over. Anyone sitting across from her could see. Atop her crossed legs, her crossed hands, the right over the left, all defense. The middle finger of the right begins, itself crossing over and exploring with its tip the cuticle of its next-door index. Finding something interesting, a tiny rough spot, she discretely raises the hand to her mouth, and with controlled pressure pushes that spot into the narrow opening she's made between superior and inferior incisors, and bites. That gets the teeth working, grinding up the morsel, while her hand returns to rest, and her thumb, a concerned but complicity nurse, rushes over to massage the wound. The rubbing, though forceful, cannot be hard enough. The morsel is chewed up too quickly. Very soon the thumb itself is chosen. Following tallman's perfunctory swipe over an existing hangnail, the opposing digit is pushed hard between the front teeth, which clamp down, and, with the thumb's furthest joint against a bicuspid for a lever, her whole right hand stiffens and twists out from the wrist, like a small salute. This is a more successful tear, freeing a gradual, but unmistakable drop of blood.

So it goes. The thumb must be sucked a bit to stanch the blood, which eases the tension some, but soon she's at work on tallman himself, her accomplice and source of intelligence, who is apparently not exempt from the universal punishment.

I don't mean to draw out the anxiety. I've always found her body language fascinating. It's edgy and vulnerable. I'm a little sorry it's come to this. Surely that's why I'm taking so long looking over her files. Not at all kind, with her sitting there. She knows what's up, and I've read over everything here more than once. Frequent tardiness, here it is, documented. Not very focused, I guess. Can't seem to meet deadlines, and often needs to go back once something's done, to repair it. Just not a very good worker, but that's hard to quantify. I haven't quite got the language down yet. Maybe that's why I'm taking so long.

My eyes on the files on the desk in front of me. Hers, too, though in a gaze. The sound of her stockings rubbing together, as she recrosses her legs.

Or my own hand on my inner thigh. I should remove it, let it stay there a moment. The drowsy swell. Between the incipient speaker and the spoken to, a child in polymorphous glee. Standing over the fallen girl, even as the teacher strides up. Irrelevant brute, a grown woman, I could not have seen her coming up behind me, though I anticipated her angry hand on my shoulder, turning me around. My defense is no defense, my gaze unfocused, my fingernail between my teeth as she scolds me. The pleasure of release, of hitting the girl who'd teased me, of knocking her down. Biting down. An atmosphere all bickering, all children tense in spreading conflict and me the focus, relieved with a punch. The flock suddenly lifts, startled.

Chewing. The little shred of cuticle flesh resisting deliciously. All in an instant attending the harsher blow of words, of punishment.

But any word can be a seed. You've got to defy words of consequence, the ones that mean to take your life from your control. Subject them to the doubt all language scuttles under. They will resist; they will twist in you.

They. The two of them. Man and woman. They worked on me for weeks, gathering the courage to cast me out. Mine was the unstable utterance, all potential outside known relation, the third that came invited, then stayed too long. Talk and talk, I would talk toward some undefined climax, but never express love, or even attraction. Sam and Lila wanted, finally, the words to do their proper job, to define a distance, to expel me. This is not their problem. They are, at the beginning and end, man and woman, suspended in the risk that hides in the next fold or crevice of skin. They have determined their ease. Imagine her moving slowly with her tongue down the dividing line of hair on his belly; he leaning back, his finger curious at the folds of her vagina. Their eyes are open; their eyes are closed. They are complete. But none of us had known their intentions. How much of them arrived with their groans and squeals, down the bare hallway to the door they'd given me, next to theirs? How else were they to invite me in?

This child came into their lives a bit too soon. I came as an adolescent: all misdirected, useless beauty. I did not speak to language. My desires were absolute and contradictory. My attraction to the woman was a pure brook, to the man a swelling wave. It was all flattery to them. Not enough to divide, nor to cement them. Mine is a speech limited by speech itself. A speech that fails in the equation of power and lust. A scrap of torn cloth, the rubbing together of stockings, a vulnerable glance, the shredded, dispossessed erotic. They cannot be held. They must be seized, torn out, and forced to submit. A man is civilized only so far as he accepts this fact. A boy comes too quickly to violence. Or watches it occur. A boy cub has no power.

Poor baby blue, all pouched and pampered by his ma, took drowsy to the blue, the blue hill side, the berries there to find. And blue, poor baby blue, the blue, blue berries in the very hot sun dud pick and pick, his mama by. He ate his fill, until, until his head did fill, and buzz, the buzzing bee did glide, and down he lay, his mom preoccupied. A could did pass. And pass alike a mam bear, her baby bear, to likewise pick, and eat, and stumble on, the afternoon so lazy by. So lazy bear babe wandered off her mam bear yet unaware, the field so blue, so sweet and warm, her baby done. The other side in shade a sleeping baby blue, and little bear did wander there, and lie. Fair clouds continued passing by, till mamas two at once in panic cried, they cried, their children absent in the wreath of vetch, and out of sight. Their simultaneous cries did fetch, not kids, but eyes, a pair of eyes in fear, distrusted species nigh. A cloud stood frozen in the sky. Blue animus unfurled, prepared to fight, defend, to die. That frozen cloud came softening, as children two at once came stumbling, stumbling out a shady lea, and parting for their mother two did turn a moment, facing each to each, good bye.

Some whimsy in my head at times confronts a messenger, confutes a message clearly given. I'm not listening. Bud and George stifling a laugh as I enter the elevator. Mark ignoring my greeting at the coffee station. Squeezed into clothing that's too sharp and too confining, their words forced out in little belches of instinct. All the brilliant thinking, all the hard work, go begging without instinct. You get a reputation. I'm the one who watches, sees nothing, and in return for being allowed to watch, forgo respect. Give me a dirty job to do. Keep me out of the loop. Keep it secret. George, for instance, I'm sure has slept with one of the secretaries. Who couldn't see that? And what does she think about it? And what do I? And what am I to do when the boys gang up and go hunting? I work here, after all. Give me a gun. Sacrifice is the name of the game. I've got to make a living.

Keep up appearances. Learn the language. My own tongue is a woman. She is a playmate, a squealer, and a liar. Not to be believed. A child can't distinguish between a fiction and a lie. But I'm not a child. Even my own words, expressing my own frustrations, seem theatrical to me. This is power. I can do this. For the first time, I notice the length of her stocking, her thigh exposed beneath a short skirt, above her nervous hands. I cannot help but look at them. They are beautiful.

A typical scene: It's a quiet morning on Croskey Street. One by one the row houses open up. Mothers, father, going off to work, the older kids to school. Here comes a father, bursting out the front door and through the tiny yard, growling in play like a bear, carrying his young boy, kicking and screaming, also playful, under his arm. At the gate, he sets him down, "Got t'go t'work! You protect mommy." He leaves, striding up the sidewalk, and the boy dawdles a moment in the front yard. His attention is caught by a spasm in a clump of grass near the neighbor's wall. It's the pigeon. He'd forgotten about it. He thought it would be dead by now. Last night, before his daddy came home, he'd broken its legs with a trowel. Then he'd held it tight, inexplicably sad at the loss of a friend. He'd meant to care for it. Now he couldn't touch it, didn't want to look at it. They carry disease, his mom had said. He took a piece of burlap that was sitting there, and put it over the bird. Then he went inside.

COLONY

9/11/01

Naturally, I can't openly express my doubts about the people who live under the lake. Each year their observance becomes a bit more ornate, and the numbers of residents who claim to have seen them — including my own sister! — grows. The Mayor, and members of the town council, sensing political advantage, eagerly participate. I abhor that kind of hypocrisy, but I also recognize the need for collective absolution that is at work in the myth. I've never heard anyone criticize it publicly, and with my employment an outgrowth of this same illogical nonsense, I certainly won't be the first to do so.

That employment involves the removal of the corpses of the debased and executed. Hanne carries them bodily, with neither assistance nor device. Not an attractive job, but one for which he exerted all available influence, including a referral from his sister's husband, who has business dealings with the police, to secure. Because of their extreme isolation in a mountain valley, the people of Hanne — nearly all males are given the name of the town itself — distrust and fear the craggy limits of their vision and their influence. Hanne is among the few who have gone beyond these boundaries, and then only by beating back his fear with singular purpose, to dispose of the bodies of the condemned.

Crimes punishable by public stoning: theft of chattel, diversion or damming of water flow, abuse or misrepresentation of authority, misrepresentation of tare weights, excessive pugnacity, physical or mental debility. Crimes punishable by disembowelment: murder, concealment of a corpse, bestiality, failure to report, arson, false identity. Crimes punishable by breaking on the wheel: flight, misrepresentation of seed, poaching, unauthorized gaming, deviant devotions, homosexuality or transvestitism. The agency of death has many guises, some more painful or humiliating than others, but all fetching the same result. However prolonged or inventive, the course of each punishment runs from elation and curiosity through the mechanical repetition of blows to dumb disappointment at the Coroner's confirmation of death. The body is suddenly a mystery among us. The people shuffle from the square, and the Master of Executions calls for me.

When Hanne looks into the lake he does not see the water. Water is threatening at its surface and in its depth, but in the end it is only water, and Hanne is its precondition.

I feel I am at some disadvantage as the Bearer of the Remains of the Condemned, since I have no direct knowledge of the people who live under the water. Their story, embellished over succeeding generations, contains enough suffering to soften the wide-spread deprivations of our townspeople, and to justify the severity of our laws. According to these proliferating myths, the ware of the lake is barely water, so crowded has it become with the flesh of a subaqueous population. These are people much like ourselves, may even be, according to some, our very selves, torn from our meager, breathing lives and plunged into the lake. The greatest horror attributed to these cursed souls is that they cannot drown. They strain perpetually toward the surface and the air above it, but they cannot sufficiently rise.

On any given evening at dusk the townspeople gather, each absorbed in his own trouble, to gaze from the dock or grassy cliff into the lake. No one speaks. By some collective agreement sightings are kept quiet until later, when around home fires or pub tables they are reported in awed tones to stern confirmations. I often join these vigils and subsequent testimonials. It's easy to blend in, to stare or nod with the group. But I have never seen other in the lake water than my own reflection.

I have watched myself in this way for several years, and have seen myself evolve from a nervous teen to a confident and handsome young man. Many are handsome, I know, but none is as handsome as I. My body is mine completely, solid, agile, roped around with muscle at shoulder and thigh. It does not belong to the lake. And while I must conceal my admiration for my own reflection, everyone knows that I am the Bearer of the Executed, and a certain display of pride is permitted, no, required of my station. I am respected and feared, so no one suspects that my pride is more in my own appearance, and not some silly loyalty to those who dispense justice.

There can be no dependence without person. Hanne is not the wavering image that he sees in the water. He lacks intuition. Each time he inhales, the sky expands, and wherever he walk the predators flee and a safe pathway is established. His caution shies beneath that caption. The world, he thinks, is his alone, because he is that rare thing, a boundary-crosser. Self-contained he moves abroad, a colony within him. What is there in this colony, beautiful Hanne, that corrupts?

Gray cloud above the lake
skimming the surface
impenetrable surface
darkness of the lake
striations of silver on the surface of the lake
viscosity of the lake
unexpected terminus
sameness
unwanted terminus
confusion of direction
difficulty of movement
dense crowd
myself too near
detesting myself
how the living bodies bloat to fill the water

Perpetual twilight on the side of the mountain. The course is steep and unmarked. Bend under the weight of the load to seek a balance point between the scapula and the spine. The deltoid moves, weight shifts. Right triceps stretches on the humerus in reaching to grip the left posterior ankle tendon, while extending the left forearm across the carotid triangle to seize the left pectoral. The neck not yet stiff, head lolling. In this way the left parietal plate the occipital gently or roughly tapping to the cadence of the bearer articulates its samenesses and its differences, those of a man, admirable or criminal, an outlaw. Two men as one, the center pole bracing, standing, bending, with great effort, standing, moving forward. Pressure of vertebrae grinding on the latissimus dorsi. Shifting, hefting a mass that is either one man, or both, but one determined to go beyond, to prevail and so to purge the colony of its impurities.

Where I end this dead one begins. His weight and his direction are mine. We are the only ones. What does he know? A liquid leaks from under his arm and down my flank. I cannot see it, but I feel it. His arm flops stiffly over my shoulder and the back of his hand scrapes the rock outcropping to our left. He is over there. I am coming toward him. He is handsome, handsomely dead. He has a great secret, and his weight reminds me that I, too, have a secret. I will show him my secret. When it is just him and me, I will show him.

* * *

Thorlon 29 has lost host. Loss of host cannot be attributed to climate or alien pathology, but to hostility of host community. This collective hostility deserves further analysis, but does not effect suitability of landmass Camen, Planet 3 for habitation. Thorlon continue seeking other hosts once decay of present host sufficient launch. Identity of Thorlon 29 has not been compromised in loss of host.

An infestation varietal 29 Qat, Thorlon has no specific physical dimension. Reproduction is host-dependent, and is initiated and sustained by host mentality deviation from predominant social mores. Requisite host have distinct nervous system, sighted. Thorlon divagate insensate, enter host with light, then multiply and expand colony according to host logical pattern.

Necessarily deviate host syntax establish Thorlon interstitially grade to dominate. When bloom in colony adversarial to language, perverse speech, feces. Small, silver disks at casual angles falling.

Contradictory capable host imbue solitary collectivity capable disbelieve harm to law utterance gain form. Suspense widely, deviation in coded particulars criminal. Articulation equate nonconform extracorporeal pleasure. Joy in mind, physical event laughter.

The husk decays. The colony waits.

* * *

A balanced predation sums up harmony at the edge of the worm field and out, beyond what's cleared.

Caution, gentleness and silence prevail, save for those times of unalloyed urgency, day or night, seized by and seizing each species. If you are reading this, you can't know these things. Your moment of consciousness is ringed by an assurance that the kingdom continues virtually uncorrupted beyond your reach. You pause in the field, lean on your shovel, listen. Feel the gradual concession of your own body to tiny cankers, microbes blistering in open sores, live, rashes and eczemas, parasites. This awareness instills a calm, a renewed acceptance of the work before you, that it will not end and that you will. You will continue to work in the interim, or you will not, either way, toward a terrible, guaranteed end, beyond which the work will go on without you. These occupants, these scabs and bugs, these will likewise fail, feeding on your flesh through their short cycle, or until somehow purged and succeeded. So the pause is delicious. It is perverse. You are not in the place represented by your body. The body below your body has lost sensation. It is a catalogue of familiar insults, a relic. Its memories are tribal, exponents of a many-footed dance you know but you can no longer perform. Grace of giving up. Pare down to the thought, the precedent thought which continues after you are gone. Pare now, now, that's the paradox. The thought is antecedent, but depends upon the moment, which is always immediately past. Fix on that thought that is not a thing. How long can you keep this up? You are dying, or next to it, exhausted. Put down the shovel, the pen, the implement. Let the implement speak for itself. You cannot hold all thoughts in your mind at once and so you try to focus on one. One elusive. No one thing save what perception's discriminating requires. Tire of this. Drop the shovel and fly off. A common housefly has more sense. It flies directly to the strongest odor and it will not be put off. It busies itself about the ears of its opponent. Its retreats are rapid, of short duration, and followed by redoubled attacks. The fly cannot rest. Nothing can be quick enough. Speed and surprise are its offense and defense. And if it stops to rest a beak or tongue will surely eat it. So the fly has no home, but had it a home that place would be a miniature cavern, a tiny mountain hall all honeycombed with windowless fly-sized rooms whose dense black and gray ceilings and walls would drip with heat and offal. The fly would only come outside to mate, to perform that elevated dance that mingles determination and fertility. Don't forget decay, the fecund places to feed the next generation. The continents are no longer virgin. These days the corporate state depends upon its client states, their civil wars, epidemics, genocides and dynasties of terror. Ripe to rotting. See what they produce.

The Amputated Toe

Cuneiform Press

2005

Here comes the Actor, the unredeemed failure. For a bit of nothing he invites us to abuse him. He carries in his pocket a little thing he calls performance, like a handkerchief he wears on his head. Come to think of it, I've never seen him without it.

The world is hemmed in on both sides by dimming memory, and on both sides by paint and cardboard. Above by light unlimited by tinker birds and chicken wire; below, the boards, the awed assembly. The world is infinite, yet with one gesture the world will go away.

We can see that the Actor is ridiculous. He is immature and vain. But rather than ridicule, we give him our attention. And if his art is slightly flawed, his acting just a tad unconvincing, we watch that much more closely. So much depends upon his success, we feel, more than he knows.

In our big empathic jar we have placed the following: dependence, catharsis, identity, consumption, I don't understand, resolution, alienation, will, decline to doubt, and spectacle.

Six cornets: a fanfare for nothing. Do you like my skirt of blue tulle, my green shirt, my tattoos? I am your brother, your brother's brother. I am slippery. There is no one left for me to be but you. Don't you agree? You thought so before I did. I haven't thought so, not yet. But I may be persuaded.

A man appears, dressed as an appendage. You've been waiting for the toe to show up. But if you refer to your program, you'll see that this is not the toe, but Mr. Tumescer. It's an easy mistake; the red pulse and heat, anyone could think it indicates infection. What's more, Mr. T is known for his aggressiveness. He has no subtext, no subtlety. Hey, Mr. T, you're looking swell! He's coming this way, dragging his testicles across the floor, pulling hairy dust along with them. Don't you feel sorry for him? I do.

The action takes place quickly. This is called "the element of surprise." The players are surrounded by a horde of players who apparently do not realize that they are players. Chaos ensues, with its attendant cacophony, which we are left to decipher. The effort this requires threatens us with a descent into exhaustion. I don't know about you, but the job of making sense of hubbub is taxing, and I'd welcome a rest.

The history of amity and procreation is recorded only in issue. History proper concerns itself with destruction. Bomb and flame, saw and pick, the landscape is torn and molded, yet the moss and weedy blooms prevail. The sharp is softened and wanders like a lost child who has given up finding his way. Every thing speaks, the wound most eloquently, for if the body is a landscape and every crevice whistles in its wind, then the unhealed wound is an adit, a mouth that won't be silenced.

This wound takes its confidence from its power to inspire fear. If you have never seen it or have only heard it described in a story, then it is possible to put it out of your mind. But once you have heard what this wound has to say, you are changed. So long as the wound is there before you, in your mind, it eclipses all memory and optimism. It is a great loneliness. It speaks obsessively of absence, which is a speech without object. It takes no solace in healing, makes no reference to injury.

Its story begins with its child, which it claims to have loved. How can a wound have a child? Well, it was not always a wound, of course. The wound was born of an insult. Where healthy flesh had stood, now is a wound, its aspirations reduced to becoming scar. That earlier time of true aspirations, of creativity and productivity, has become a yellowed lamination. The wound is a new kind of sensory organ, overriding the vocabulary of compassion, and so its love of the child is only a word without meaning.

A toe, particularly a grand toe, is a necessity for hiking. It is the pivot, balance, forbearance, the difference between burden and delight. What's more, this particular hike winds steeply up the rocky creek bed, along a path which frequently requires bending at the waist or hopping from rock to rock across the charming water. Who is this Hiker? And what is her appearance? On her back she carries a sleeping, swaddled passenger. Is this her child? A child she has stolen? She seems too young a girl to have a baby of her own. Where is she headed, is she running away, and if so, away from what or whom? Answers to these questions might make an interesting story, but they are not relevant to this one. But how to proceed without that toe?

With or without the toe, the Hiker must occasionally rest. Here's a spot. The woods are so thick the sun rarely penetrates, but here the moss and shepherd's purse crowd upon a rock to make a cushion, and a fallen log support for a weary back. Before she rests, the Hiker cautiously removes the precious package from her back, chooses a firm branch, and hangs it there like a cocoon.

Odd, the exhausted Hiker thinks as she sinks down, what unusual flora here about. Tiny mushrooms in the shape of coronets, and lichens colored lavender and cerulean. A cold breeze passes over the place, and the Hiker senses she is not alone. She starts. A figure, half boy, half deer, stands as if interrupted while drinking, across the brook.

No one speaks. And then the Hiker speaks.

"Hans, I know frol bachner. Cam delit follow me?"

"Farbeit anro mine, Katrina."

"Mus ridicular, tan kleigh parnock. Gym freebold the forest."

"Then I will bredst fort. Clad peelon."

"Frad deemes, Hans. Ich simuel faster, smarter, surer…

But the deer has stopped listening. He jumps over the creek and charges toward the girl, knocking her over as he runs past, up the rocky bank and gone into the thicket. The Hiker rights herself, then stands. The lichen has lost its magical hue, and there is no sign of the deer. With renewed urgency, the Hiker knows that it is time to move on.

Once the throng of players has left the stage, we are left with two, a reasonable cast. Seated at a table is a woman, though it is difficult to tell that is what she is because she is just a stick figure. Simple, undivided lines for her arms, her legs and torso, but on her poorly drawn round head a crop of curls pays homage to femininity.

On the table before her, flexing blindly on a platter, a household spirit given a name, much like the ribbed pupa of a moth discovered by a curious and inconsiderate child in a corner of the barn in early spring, its resident caterpillar only halfway metamorphosed into a moth. But this twitching lump is far bigger than the word pupa would suggest, looking to weigh in at half a stone, and when it stretches out, about the size of a football. More than this cannot be said about it, as it is as undefined as the very work of theatre in which it finds itself.

Who will play opposite this fragile, stick-like figure of a woman? Whose voice is all inaudible resonance, rattling the bottles on the shelves and pressing on the scalp? Shadow without substance, angles without planes. Whose speech even as it is spoken is a memory? From inside the one who hears, an ache for the present. From inside, a turning of the back.

UNCOLLECTED POEMS

THE WHAT TO WHOM

for JML

Hello! May I
Crm b light poem b
Seducing mind s mind

Evva stone, a tick
I random's bitt'n
Wits task

A hire powr? M'n
Question: the text
Roll'm thd's requisite, gravity:

:aleatory. M'a
yrs tween lack
n'a brtch's, t hap'ns

universally, t takes a poet
to make an absence
sing

thick
tongued intllect
a solve

nt dance I
rddy here pr
pared fr

"U"
:ommen
end.

Fugue

FUGUE

for Jono Schneider

This time I won't even consider leaving; I'll simply go.

Here are Paul and Nila, warm and stuffy in their kitchen in disagreement, of which the foundation is stale agreement. No wonder the equation, fear and love. Paul my old buddy from high school days, with whom I drank and defamed the Pope, standing puzzled, fisted, unable to move forward or back, inertia forever to determine his course, if he is lucky. Dungarees, plaid flannel, work boots. By her rights Nila sits this one out, her thighs spread on the wood seat beneath denim, her glass of red within reach. Nothing happens.

No, I don't mean to shake their good intentions. I'm just going to make my move. I say so.

As their tired argument needs relief, they unify in shock and admonition toward me. What will you do, out there, alone, if things go wrong, asks Paul, the surrender of his will apparent in the question. But you've made so much progress here with us, pipes adumbrated Nila. I can almost hear their collective jaw drop, as if the cartouche of their World depicted savages and dragons.

A door is a simple mechanism, yet steeped in lore and symbol.

Nothing is uneventful to the man recently self-declared. My step light on the cobbles I emerge amid a throng. A warm day, the first of days, this is all. From either side of the street the houses lean, five, seven storeys, I lose count, pink, blue, yellow, green, dormers, cupolas, porticos, corbel, cornice and caryatid, baroque architecture, From out these doors the people pour, achatter, their clothing garish to my taste, cuffs and collars loose and brightly colored. All are in a hurry. I, too, am in a hurry, to nowhere in particular l. I am too stimulated. I tell my feet to find a rural road.

Art is not to be trusted.

A day's arduous passages abbreviated, society and its symptoms gone for the rustic landscape, my eyes, ear, and heart find the lark, but my wayward foot finds the scorpion. The weather warm and the injury minor, I prepare my convalescence on the side of the road. Conveniently a stream nearby, for to drink and to soak the afflicted appendage. Scorpion bites are rarely fatal. A nuisance, but a sore one.

Troubled by delirium.

Without cover exposed to all elements I spot the sun, to which no adjective attaches, at six o'clock, at two, at setting. Light rain, then more sun. Procession of days, of shadows. This is enough. Yet here walks a lady. Or I should say she glides.

She ministers to me in silence. She digs a bitter toot, which she boils, distills, decants, doses. Her hand is steady, her breasts pendulous above mine, supine. Her gaze and breath emissaries from the province of well-being. I feel that I am far, wandering my unique, uncomplicated territory, and she is a tether to the near world. What gentle song she makes I cannot distinguish from that of the nearby stream. Sonorous Nature soothes me in my distraction. The squirrels natter endlessly, over nothing. Surely there are enough branches and enough tender buds for all. But there is a great commotion among them. It seems some of their number have been found scattered and lifeless in the field. No sign of mauling by the barnyard dog, no evisceration, as the hawk would do. Two this very morning, sleek and dead. It is enough to cause a general panic. In all but one, that is. This one recalls the raid upon the refuse pit two nights hence. He and his acquaintance stole upon the scene to find fresh garbage, yes, and more, a fine white powder. Let the partner eat that. It wasn't long the eager tool contorted, twitched, commenced to run in circles, then to stop. Our protagonist was impressed. As noted, during this warm season there is no shortage of natural feed, but all the same the wood's a bit too crowded for our buddy. Next he steals alone, and wipes a few choice kernels in that special dust, and these he places where he knows the other squirrels congregate. Is he not innocent, to want to trim the herd? But he is not content at this. He knows the branch where recently a nest was filled with naked infants. Their protector dead, they will be unprotected. Tonight, he will pay a visit.

There is nothing so persuasive as a sentence that knows when to stop.

My caretaker, were she ever here, would seem to have departed. I note my pockets riffled, my wallet gone. Now I see that in the hubris of falling ill I lay me down against a rock which, despite the weather's general warmth, held in its shade the winter's chill and damp. So my recovery is retarded, the scales slow to fall. I force myself up and about.

The out-of-doors tilts larger, the fresh air burns my lungs, my legs weak, step wobbles. It's time to pack up camp.

Have I forgotten my direction? Had I one? There is cruelty in the present tense, as in the first person. A damp yellow field, sloping gradually to the unpaved road where I stand, then up more precipitously behind me. But of course I cannot see that. Scattered throughout the field boulders large and small. A stream would break the monotony of this picture, but my thirst is quenched and I have no more use for a stream. What I would like now is a conversation, to discuss the situation, the likelihood of rain, the proper direction to walk, all things tangled with a future, but sensible exchange requires a separate consciousness, rival or ally, and here is none.

Contradiction is bliss. Self-contradiction is orgasm.

Thus begins my life as a couple. I find I've an other. I want to be precise. My other is small, small enough for me to dominate, yet large enough to draw my affections.

This other is annuliform, pert cetaceous, vaporous. Without access to a genderizing pronoun this other continually fulminates before me. Kaleidoscopically before me this other my weaknesses my strengths exploits. My little machine accelerates at promise, grows sluggish at disappointment. I want to be addressed, feel I am so. Unfortunately, I cannot hear as a subway train rushes past, filling our tunnel with its insistence. But it feels so good to utilize the first person plural I beg reiteration.

Addressed, answered, and accosted, am I.

"Your eyes alone, and not even they, but the brilliant pinpoints at their centers, would have been enough to pull me from the mass of undistinguished things. I multiply your difficulty and your pleasure. You open your mouth and I crawl in, down, you vomit me forth. I am silken. I take you by your hand into the darkness. My hand fills your awareness. It moves on the tender parts. I find your secrets and you relinquish them to me. Now we are forever outside. We seek obscurity, knees deep in the subterranean aquifer. At times I lead, at times you, forever forward without plan, this our singular enjoyment. I dance on your tongue. I bring you manna from the forests of Brazil. We are alone together among multitudes. They couple and twist as on a living tapestry. Are we, or are we not? Incorporeal fear pursues us. Time after time our escape is narrow. We arrive here, in a mall room, a plank cubicle with one doorless door and two windowless windows. You tire of running, sink to the mattress on the floor. Tropical air does not revive you. I panic at your fatigue. I run from that place into the woods, shouting, wasting my breath. Ocean waves send quick glints of sunlight to me through the trees as I run. Worthless detail. I am exhausted. There is no one to help me."

Without past, without future, claiming nothing.

As I was born. Consistently so. I travel my occult landscape looking for the face poorly remembered. The word poorly defined. I am in the chair by the window. Paul visits me. It's my last chance, he says. I don't look at him. I know it is not really him. The surface of the corn is dulled with a light dust. A dream inside a dream. How great the insults. I stride, I fly. Flight is one trajectory, fatigue another. These lines cross, but not in the present. I manage with all my strength to push the future before me. It fools me. It is light and insubstantial, yet I give it all my effort. I am sweating, or fevered. I lose and lose, called memory, behind as light as what's before me. There is a little boat before me. I am so tired of hidden meaning. From now on meaning will be plain. It is an aluminum boat, a rowboat for two, though there is just me. The shore is of shiny gravel, the water gentle, lapping, sinking into the stones. I lie down in the bottom of the boat. Narrow, the gunwales loom over, enfolding. Softly rocking. I am sleeping.

> Swim little fish,
> swim to me.
> Swim little fish
> from the bottom of the sea.

A word about the author: Wasn't that a tidy ending? Now you can go back to your business. What is your business, anyway? I'm very interested in you. Let me get closer to you so you can speak directly into my good ear. Does this bother you? Am I giving off an unpleasant odor? I've tried everything to get rid of it. Lotions, soaps, baths, powders. Do you have any suggestions? If you say it, I'll do it. I'm very fond of you, you know.

LASH OF

finds dream through the window
moving car.

stationary seat lets beams enter, pierce
and pass,
do
their indelible erasing.

small luminous night.
so many black men,
dark green men
wild in the sky,
shred the image.

SNAPSHOT

Archilochus'
steady shaft

or Sappho: "Lock
your shield to mine in the siege…"

John
from a wave in the otherwise insignificant sea

shouts:
"Found it!"

brother, brandishing the snorkeling tube
we'd allowed, in a lapse, the Caribbean to claim.

(from a letter to Eli Goldblatt, 31 July, 1985, Full Moon Day, Nagua)

Gradually I remember
details, details only, and not
the whole, horrible crime.

The earth beneath the grass beneath my feet
all solid, all of water, giving way suddenly

exhilarated by guilt

rising, as to my knees. The low,
dark space I'll later call "a dirty birth"
closes as I crawl,

evidence assembled, in need only
of a key,

vanishing. Transport
is the subject, how the body moves
by its own means, not mine. Quick
to pull a prone weight through a hall
by fingerholds, up stairs, another hall,
exhausted, other hallways, vast segmented

fear a telling

as a smile in a re-
membered department
where I am led
by one himself
out of a maze, accuser.

COFFEE WITH KIM

sick so often

live forever, young psychotic
who is ninety, he's
her lawyer for our survival
lose our loved ones
resurrected

call their names, then
she kills them all

touching their breasts
from the grave, pronounced dead.
You can work on them sexually.
To rouse somebody

puts me in furnaces,
puts me in oceans,
on fire
my face covered with knife wounds
burns.

If she has me chained down, I break out.

I have the word from people who have been dead.
I've survived those horrible feelings

except
can't sleep at night

PASSION

Cut
a ma han dig'n
t'enter her tain, 's blood
w'sand balled up'n FREED
Murky water, gossamer air,
were't n t f'th m'nute channel
sbloom i'th d'tested flesh
all pulse push an anx't'd be
a thing learned, a hawk's
yellow eye. N'how
she'g nores me! N
diffrnt a losses scarlet
tress run runny t'in
g'netic tread b'tween
's scap'd a me tests.
Piss't weh, whose? Ifn't
hers mine's a vapor
t'd'fend. Suit'v anger,
impt nt corpus w dout'sm
buddy pits'er all awares
mocky t'old wut dear?
Her face. The summer light
on's tourn'n air cor
r'rupts abt ages worse
wraps a lap p'bout
t'pock a plain 'spress
grace. S'sa prick'n'a
pact! Dn outs th greedy
s'nsa p tches hyu
shoe f'they own ens. L'a
ma narri fist g'daw
n'air inna rest g's n'
a deep earn skin on ice.
Mna fail s's'duce'm b'
th' "extraordinary t
verge" un tch d'strain, s
wung n'rgn's weigh
tol histry's quck shallow
cors. Comm'n love. Sr
fs'x change, m n f o'
f'fludes a bz t'bodly
sores. Om frail, m
breaths fain t'age. Fls
well t'deps'un own s'sex

saw flash ‘nna interstices
osso shl prob’ty. Cpling freely
t’up it rect m’saturate
change w’d sire, s’
natch l’no?

BROADCAST

of black a browning
field appears
mapping pure dance
breezes skirts and
fertile
bless a sudden central oak

and dark. House
ages at once.
too close this brother our
heart insists
i know i know
prefocal parts are skin
brown as mine, again
words are wrong.

brown shakes back
all leaves a breeze
of this which
indicates departure

OH WHEN THE SAINTS

after the death of my Father

One solid boat vessel in an ice-jerked sea of this season of melting water and fingers as chicken bones and melancholy. The press of lap hands, bulky houses of women with unwrapped hope: tasty.

St. Matthew meets St. David meets St. Luke meets St. Gregory meets St. John Baptist de la Salle meets St. Francis de Sales. They might ask each other why are we here? The offerings are top notch: Cheese and Onion Pudding; Chard and Saffron Tart; Creamy Asparagus Timbale; Whole Baked Eggplants; Rhubard Fool; and Almond Pine-Nut Tart. We will work! We will feast first!

"They are only new born phobias" Take a rusty tea fro warmth. There, there, dead of night lasts too long. The kitten following us to bed with dreaming vertebrae and a tail tucked over inconsistency and buckets of sardines, marckerel, and grouper for sale. Take the flesh and line the room with illuminated bones as calligraphic warnings. "No wonder you're afraid!"

Michelangelo Buonarroti was said to have four souls. There Saints working for him. Barbara, Luke (twice) and David. There is a Last Judgment and there isn't a Last Judgment. Is it true that he is still alive in his architecture, paintings, sculpture, and poetry? The Rabbi said as much at the service. "Oh how the wind whipped through the funeral canopy then."

Stand outside the door in a crack of light. Anxious chords blanket windpipe. Always the pre-speech. "Say (mother's name)." As if you warned us of the most ferocious of hungers. "Ma is a nun, as I am."

The text is produced from the Gospel of St. Matthew. How loud did he orchestrate to be heard. Passion is placed in the sepulchre, and now with his body supine, protectors slip from the room having finished with all manners and with Father.

UNTITLED

From the silence she has filled
and from all measurement turning
space, blank space of a room enduring
promise, what is to have begun
begins, vibrant, beneath hearing.

That she distributes other airs
figures little in the composition
time has made, alternatives to freedom
falter, pale, equivocate her.

And in her transience constitute
philosophy, all that speaks in poetry
driven to light, reddening what secretly
warms the obdurate hear and keeps
in memory death's transparency

NIGHT AND DAY WILL PASS AWAY

Night and day will pass away
But love will always win
Night and day will pass away
But love will always win

Moon and stars fall from the sky
But love will always win
Moon and stars fall from the sky
But love will always win

Afterword

Founded in 1984 in Tucson, Arizona, the history of Chax Press has occupied the same years as my friendship with Gil Ott. Even before I met Gil, his editing of *Paper Air* led me to great admiration of his work, led Chax Press to some of the poets we would later publish (Jackson Mac Low, Ron Silliman, etc.), and led me to a sense that here was a poet and editor of great insight, great humility, and a marvelous sense of both reticence and dignity. When I met Gil, which was when I went to the wedding of Eli Goldblatt (co-editor of this book) and Wendy Osterweil, and spent a few nights sleeping on his floor, my expectations were met in full and beyond. I witnessed his ability to hone his life so that what mattered is what was most present, a characteristic true of his editing (of *Paper Air* and of Singing Horse Press) and his poems. While the editing obviously mattered to me, because Singing Horse books are immaculate and *Paper Air* issues always had new and key information (and eventually Singing Horse would publish my poems, as had *Paper Air* earlier), it is Gil's poems that I have come to live with over time, and which carry, for me, Gil's own profound insights, sensibility, and presence.

When Gil Ott died in February 2004, he was to have appeared in a Chax Press reading in New York City along with Jackson Mac Low, Charles Bernstein, Nick Piombino, Heather Thomas, Hank Lazer, Bob Perelman, Mark Weiss, Allison Cobb, Trace Peterson (co-editor of this book), and myself. The day became one of the saddest I have known when we heard the news that Gil had died of kidney failure. I shall never forget the ashen look on Jackson's face when I told him what had happened.

But now what I feel about Gil is what I felt early on, that I have a colleague, a friend, a fellow traveler, with whom I share a mission, a vision, a passion, a life. I feel, as always, honored that Gil was and is a part of my life, and a part of the life of Chax Press. This book is evidence of his marvelous poems, and of his being, through his friends, collaborators, and readers. I thank them all, and I particularly thank Julia Blumenreich, who most closely shared a life with Gil, shared the parenting of Willa Bea Ott, and whom I am also fortunate to count as a friend. Such friendship offers further evidence that Gil believed that our humanity is to be shared; he shared his with Julia and Willa in a most inspiring manner.

Charles Alexander
Director, Chax Press

arrive on *wave*